"YOU AREN'T ONE OF THE BOYS"

AUTHORITY IN THE
CATHOLIC PRIESTHOOD

"You aren't one of the boys"

(A priest respondent)

AUTHORITY IN THE CATHOLIC PRIESTHOOD

Noel Timms

with contributions by

Kenneth Wilson and Paul Conroy

Matthew James Publishing Ltd

First published 2001 by:
Matthew James Publishing Ltd
19 Wellington Close
Chelmsford, Essex CM1 2EE

Copyright © 2001,
The Queen's Ecumenical Foundation for Theological Education

ISBN 1 898366 70 5

Typeset in Bembo by Linda East
Cover design by Peter Robb
Printed in Great Britain by J W Arrowsmith, Bristol

Contents

Foreword Professor Jan Kerkhofs SJ	*i*
Introduction	*1*
Chapter One: THE PRACTICE OF PRIESTHOOD	*9*
Chapter Two: ORIENTATION TO THE PRACTICE OF A PRIEST	*21*
Chapter Three: ORDINATION: ROUTES AND OUTCOMES	*39*
Chapter Four: GOVERNANCE: HOLY ORDERS AND HOLY ORDERING	*71*
Chapter Five: PRIESTLY AND LAY AUTHORITY	*85*
Chapter Six: CONTROVERSIAL ISSUES FACING THE CHURCH	*101*
Chapter Seven: GENERAL CONCLUSION	*129*
Chapter Eight: THE AUTHORITATIVE CHURCH (Rev. Dr. Kenneth Wilson)	*145*
Chapter Nine: LIVING WITH TENSION (Fr. Paul Conroy)	*157*
Appendix One: THE RESEARCH TOPIC GUIDE	*183*
Appendix Two: SELECTED FINDINGS FROM AN AMERICAN SURVEY	*193*
Appendix Three: THE AUTHORITY AND GOVERNANCE PROJECT	*195*
Bibliography	*199*

Foreword

HALF A CENTURY AGO a study such as this would have been unthinkable. The priest was part of the mysterious world of the sacred. Entering into this domain with sociological methods was considered sacrilegious. The study shows that in the meantime openness in the Church and among the priests has greatly increased. This is also the case in several other European countries where similar surveys have been organised in the years after Vatican II. All reveal that priests are generally happy with their vocation, and that, at the same time, the majority of the clergy, including the older generations, is looking for more or less important changes in doctrine and discipline (as is documented in a book I have published with a team of European colleagues).[1]

The following brief considerations do not try to summarise this very interesting work. They are not more than marginal reflections by an old professor who happens to be at the same time a sociologist and a theologian.

What probably strikes me most is the fact that, once again, as many specialists in post-Vatican II developments have observed, several theologies of Church and priesthood coexist. This was also the case in the Council documents themselves. As an example, I mention the more hierarchical approach and the more 'synodal' one. The respective followers of these interpretations find arguments both in Scripture and tradition. Socio-psychological factors are surely interfering with these approaches. However, I am convinced that very often lack of theological insight and of information about Church history, as well as development of doctrine (J. H. Newman) explain the sometimes very important pastoral conclusions which somehow divide priests. I say: 'somehow', because the answers are seldom totally black or totally white. There is no profound polarisation, as we see in some European countries. But it appears that on some basic aspects of the faith (or seen as such by the interviewees) too many respondents accept rather uncritically partial interpretations or follow obediently what comes from 'above'. I mention some of these items, which are touched upon

several theologies of church and priesthood coexist

in the study: transubstantiation, the sacramental 'mark' with its 'ontological' impact, the Eucharist as a sacrifice, women priests, intercommunion, sacramental participation of divorced and remarried, the validity of Anglican orders. On all these items priests have divergent views, often based mainly upon authority and tradition; seldom on solid theologising.

Importantly, we need to update the theology of the priesthood itself. The steadily growing role of the laity in the Church, mainly as a consequence of the overburdening of the priests, resulting from their decreasing numbers and their increasing age, everywhere questions the identity of the priest. This comes clearly into the open when in his Conclusions Timms states that 'Priesthood can be viewed as sacred, as functional, and as communitarian'. Of course, different theologies are at work. The study suggests that too many priests do not find time for ongoing formation and training. This is regrettable for the simple reason that one can foresee in the near future that the (often still hidden) identity crisis will increase, as many surveys on the European continent reveal. Indeed, we are at a turning point regarding the self-understanding of the priest. He needs solid ground upon which to build his pastoral commitment and begin redefining his roles. This is particularly true in a period where many 'traditions' are in a flux and when some look back to yesterday's certainties, while others, taking into account the new socio-cultural context, want rather radical changes.

It strikes me also that many interviewees stress the Eucharist as the centre of their priestly life. Of course, celebrating the Eucharist is a core element of priestly tasks and all theologians emphasise the right of the faithful to the Eucharist. But why not raise a question about what I call 'the Sacrament of the Word'? Preaching and catechisation (of young people and of adults) are at least as important as the Eucharist. Knowledge of the Scriptures and updated theology are here essential preconditions. People have to be helped in discerning how to apply the appeal of the Gospel to the complexities of their lives as Christians and as citizens. Many lay people read more theological literature than ever before and they are questioning a too repetitive explanation of Christian doctrine. If the priest, as happens in too many European dioceses, is reduced to a 'sacramentalist', it would be a disaster. The Gospel

we are at a turning point regarding the self-understanding of the priest

shows us a Jesus who is mainly a teacher. Just like St Paul, he left the sacraments (and in the beginning they were few) to other members of the community. Preaching and teaching mean interpreting and reinterpreting. It is a prophetic gift, which in the early Church was not exceptional.

Another element in need of further research deals with authority, the general topic of this study. Several questions asked by NOP mention the role of the laity in Church government. The answers did no more than point to the top of an iceberg. When most theologians today consider the *synodal* aspect of the Church as a key challenge for modern ecclesiology, more research and reflection seem needed. In secular society (as in business, unions, schools, hospitals and of course in political parties) 'participative management' has become a rule for good leadership. The reasons are manifold. Our post-feudal and post-industrial society is changing fast. Sciences and their application (e.g. Internet) develop new kinds of rapid communication. At the same time, thanks to the democratisation of education, people are no longer willing to remain passive followers of instructions coming from above. They want a say in everything.

Though Vatican II opened – at a distance of about 35 years and still in a very timid way – some perspectives upon more consultative ways of dealing with laity, priests and bishops, the facts point too often in another direction. In many countries diocesan and national synods have been sterilised. At different levels the conferences of priests have lost their initial drive and even the most committed leaders among the member priests are seriously disillusioned. At the Episcopal level, almost everyone admits politely or in a more outspoken way, that since the 1985 Synod the Roman Curia has strongly influenced the preparatory documents, the working groups during the sessions and the final synod documents. Meanwhile, again and again, it is stressed that the Church is not a democracy. Of course, it is not. The Gospel, its Constitution, can never be changed or 'adapted' by votes. And, as in all human groupings, leadership is essential. But surely also, the Church is not an oligarchy or a monarchy. The medieval theologians and the Popes (even the authoritarian Boniface VIII) have always accepted as a rule the old statement: 'Quod omnes tangit, ab omnibus tractari et approbari debet' (What concerns everyone has to be debated and accepted by everyone).

The Church is neither a business, nor a bank nor an army. It is first of all a movement of volunteers. At all levels the members should treat one another as volunteers, putting their gifts of body and mind into the growth of this movement, where the Spirit of the Lord is the principal leader. This means that the Church is a listening community, open to the insights of all the members and trying to decipher mental and societal changes. One way of realising this communication is surely the personal dialogue of the priests, the volunteers 'par excellence', with the bishop. Another is by fostering the exchange of dreams and frustrations among the priests themselves. In the relation of priests and laity, teamwork will become the rule. It will have to be learned during the training years. Priests will become more and more facilitators, not 'above', but within the community. This does not mean that there is no need for authority, but the difference between real authority and 'clerical power' will become more explicit. I guess that the former model of the priest as a man 'set apart' will gradually disappear, as is the case in most previously quasi 'sacred' professions (such as doctors or lawyers). The priest will not lose his central role as responsible pastor, but everyone will find it normal that other team-members are really co-responsible (as is the case in the Netherlands and Belgium for 'pastoral workers' and in Germany and Switzerland for 'pastoral assistants').

is it possible to train clergy for leadership?

An important question remains: is it possible to train clergy for leadership? We have to admit that it will be very difficult to apply to the Church the methods used for secular professions to screen and train future leaders. The Church remains a very complex movement where efficiency is not a central concern and where profit making has no meaning. Most learn swimming by jumping into the pool. In a keynote address on Leadership to the English Conference of Religious in 1997, the late Cardinal Basil Hume said: "I discussed leadership with a man who had a distinguished army career and was later in life highly successful in business. Between the two of us, we decided that there were five constituents of leadership: vision, conviction, consistency, example and courage… But it is subtler than that. So, I added three: empathy, sympathy and a sense of humour. Having got *that far, I then decided to pursue my thinking about leadership. You will not be surprised to hear that for abbots there is no staff college, nor for bishops. We get no training whatsoever to be superiors. You get pushed into it, elected into it and you have to get on with it. It would be rather awful if you were trained to be a superior and much worse if you were trained to be a bishop."* And the cardinal added: *"Who wants an 'efficient bishop'?"*. With all due respect to a great man, who was a personal friend, I think that a certain training, after the appointment would be a good thing, mainly to avoid mistakes. Anyhow, the Jesuits have introduced this for their newly appointed major superiors. In the past, most curates were trained by parish priests before having to preside over their own parish. Cardinal Suenens was not afraid to introduce women into the training process.

Living on the other side of the Channel, I dare to offer a suggestion. I dream about meetings between priests from the UK and their colleagues on the Continent. Indeed, what is beginning to happen in England, Wales and Scotland is here already a daily reality. Thousands of parishes have been merged and an increasing number of parish priests are in charge of several parishes, sometimes ten and more. Many parishes are entrusted to theologically trained 'lay pastors', while at regular intervals a priest comes for the Eucharist. In more and more dioceses in the Netherlands, Germany and Switzerland an ecumenical pastoral approach has become the rule at grass root level. Meanwhile public attitudes towards the 'resigned' priests have also changed as the opinion polls are showing.

Finally, it would be interesting to compare the opinions of regularly practising Catholics with the opinions of the clergy. The conclusions of this comparison could feed diocesan meetings. This might foster the synodal character of Church life. Taking into account the findings of the three surveys organised in 1981, 1990 and 1999 by the *European Values Study* Foundation, it appears that in survey after survey most communities of Catholic believers are becoming more and more 'a little flock' on 'a narrow path'. In such a 'diaspora'-situation confidence and friendship between all involved seem the main virtues to keep hope alive for the future.

The study is an important tool for helping parishes and dioceses to 'read the signs of the times' and to prepare the Church of tomorrow, called to continue the 'aggiornamento', started by Vatican II and to develop new styles of leadership, adapted to the vision of the Gospel and the expectations of people in the third millennium.

Jan Kerkhofs SJ
Emeritus Professor Catholic University of Louvain

---

[1] *Europe without Priests?* (SCM, London, 1995)

Introduction

THIS STUDY IS BASED on two main sources. First, a survey by NOP Business commissioned by the Authority and Governance project of Queen's College, Birmingham. Second, a further qualitative analysis undertaken by the author of the tape-recorded interviews conducted by NOP Business from participants willing for their tapes to be heard under strict conditions of anonymity. In addition limited use has been made of written communications from serving priests and from others no longer permitted to minister. The Queen's Project on Authority and Governance in the Roman Catholic Church attempts to encourage as wide a circle of respondents as possible in a conversation on this crucial topic. The first publication of the Queen's Project was entitled 'From Confrontation to Conversation'. This perhaps suggests a retreat to the warm vacuity of chat, but as the philosopher who has made the notion of conversation central to his argument has remarked:

> *"As civilised human beings, we are the inheritors, neither of an inquiry about ourselves and the world, nor of an accumulating body of information, but of a conversation, begun in the primeval forests and extended and made more articulate in the course of centuries. It is a conversation which goes on both in public and within each of ourselves. Of course there is argument and inquiry and information, but wherever these are profitable they are to be recognised as passages in this conversation..."*
>
> (Oakeshott, 1962, p. 199)

NOP Business was commissioned to undertake an inquiry which would produce a report on how priests of the Roman Catholic Church, present and no longer officiating, regarded issues of authority and governance in the Church. The intention was to secure as wide a cross section of respondents as possible. Accordingly interviews were sought with seminarians, priests who have been recently ordained, serving Catholic priests (parochial), serving Catholic priests (non-parochial), bishops, and those priests who are no longer officiating in public ministry. What was

'From Confrontation to Conversation'

achieved were 65 individual face-to-face depth interviews, each lasting up to two and a half hours. The distribution of interviews and of those willing for their taped interviews to be passed direct to Queen's College is as follows:

TABLE ONE

Category of Respondent	Interviews Conducted	Tapes to Queen's
Second Year Seminarian	10	6
Recently Ordained	10	5
Serving Priests: Parochial	15	11
Serving Priests: Non Parochial	10	6
Bishops	5	-
Ordained but no longer officiating	15	12
	65	40

Participants were selected at random mainly from the Catholic Directory 1998 (England and Wales) and the Catholic Directory for Scotland 1998. The Advent Group for those no longer exercising official ministry allowed NOP to distribute a letter to members inviting participation in the Research. Of the 15 interviewed 4 had not been in active ministry for up to 5 years; 7 for between 6 and 20 years and 4 for over 21 years.

The bishops interviewed were currently in office. Newly ordained priests included those who have completed their training and were ordained in 1996 or 1997. Because of the random selection of participants, three of the newly ordained priests who participated were former Anglican clergy. Most of the newly ordained in the study were serving as assistant priests in parishes. Those not working as assistants were divided between parish priests and non-parochial priests working as chaplains, priests in retreat houses and so on. (To ensure confidentiality not all positions were recorded in the NOP Report). The distinction between the two groupings may appear of limited use when it is noted that many of those interviewed in a non-parochial capacity were also serving a parish. However, as we shall see, we can examine the extent to which the different experiences of those with major responsibilities without the parish led to differences of judgement about some of the important issues facing the Roman Catholic Church. We should also note that of the total of 25 parish and non-parochial priests 8 were ordained before 1963.

At this point reference should be made to difficulties involved in finding a short description of those no longer officially exercising the office of priest. The NOP survey referred to them as 'resigned', but this may appear a misleading gloss on a final act that was taken after considerable pressure. It may also seem to detract from a belief in ministry that continues, albeit in some cases as husband and father, after 'resignation'. Those who no longer exercise the office of priest believe, as we shall see, strongly in the continuing spirituality of the priest. References in any commentary in this study to this group will use a phrase such as 'no longer officially ministering', whilst the shorthand 'resigned' will identify the source of the relevant quotation. Interviews were conducted by NOP between November 1998 and June 1999.

Table Two indicates the location of these interviews.

TABLE TWO

Location of Interviews	Number of Interviews
London and South East	22
North of England	15
Midlands	11
Scotland	10
Wales	7
	65

Interviews with seminarians were conducted at seminaries in England and Scotland. All participants were asked questions on the same topics with appropriate variation for certain groups. The range of questions asked and the kind of variation required can be seen in the NOP Topic Guide in Appendix One.

The second source for this study of Roman Catholic Priests derives from a study of the transcripts made of the 40 tapes concerning which respondents gave permission for further analysis. This makes two specific contributions. First, it enables a richer illustration of the interview material, as priests and others, attempt to give answers about the motivation and purpose of their *the network of words*

work which many of us would find difficult to articulate. It also illuminates the extent to which the network of words found across the interviews – community, service, ministry, parish, leadership and so on – conceal significant differences at a conceptual level. Second, the further analysis helps in the understanding of an individual's responses taken as a whole, the extent to which such dichotomies as theory-practice, ideal-actual, spiritual-temporal are used by participants to make their worlds intelligible, and the extent to which they strive for consistency.

If, as the introduction to Optatam Totius states, *"the desired renewal of the whole Church depends in great part upon a priestly ministry animated by the spirit of Christ"*, it must be important to examine how this ministry is understood by those who have exercised it in the past and those who continue to do so. Pope John Paul II's concern with specifying the identity of the Catholic Church accompanies a wish to establish clearly the distinguishing identity of the Catholic priesthood. Do priests agree about the constituents of this identity? The English Charter for Priestly Formation endorses the view that *"The priestly office... is today carried out in an entirely new situation, which comes to light as a result of humankind's new needs and from the nature of modern civilisation."* Do priests see any ways in which these new needs make new demands on their 'leadership'? Do they see that 'changed situation' also applies within the Church? As Duffy (1996) has argued *"... the Tridentine moment is passing, perhaps has already passed... we do not need or at any rate no longer want the sort of clerical guru which Trent set itself to produce... we are confronted with an urgent need to re-imagine the ordained priesthood, as the Counter-Reformation re-imagined and reinvented it."*

Looking ahead

This study of those in the active priesthood, those who have left and those hopeful of joining will tap an indispensable source for exploring the possibilities of such re-imagining. The present work, which does not follow precisely the order of the interview guide, explores seven topics. It begins with a consideration of the practice of priesthood and the rhetoric used by priests to describe and explore it. It is important at this early stage to be clear that rhetoric refers not to verbal fireworks but to significant words in public

the rhetoric used by priests

argument used to state a position and convince an audience (Billig, 1987). Two terms seem particularly significant to the priests who have been interviewed, service and a working idea of 'church'. Each term, as we shall see, covers several distinct conceptions, and 'service' jostles with priestly status and the common suspicion of those who live for others – *"you can tell the latter by their hunted look."* There are also less exalted notions that can be used to make the practice of priesthood intelligible to practitioners and others – parish manager, ministry as functional, as professional, hopefulness and feedback. These are considered in the second chapter.

The third chapter seeks to explore how it is that respondents have come to be engaged in the practice of priesthood. This involves examining the reasons they gave for becoming a priest and the idea of vocation or calling. In what ways is the special vocation of a priest distinguished from the call of Christ to all Christians? Were the present notions of service and of Church what the respondents expected to put into their own practice and have their expectations been met? Finally, this chapter examines the views of priests on their years of seminary formation, and their ideas for change and for formation that continues beyond the seminary.

On the basis of the present practice of a priest, and of their views of their preparation for such practice, we turn in Chapter Four to the role of the priest in the governance of the Church. Respondents discussed this in the precise terms of Canon Law, and in terms of general administration. In each sense there appeared to be satisfaction with church government, but no sense was conveyed that issues of government could be dismissed as of secondary importance. (See 'A Duel between Two Cardinals', The Tablet, 29th January, 2000, p.125.) Those most critical of current Church government could been seen as those nearest the action, bishops and those no longer in official ministry. The former were more circumspect than the latter.

Chapter Five considers opinion on the division of authority between priests and lay people. This involves re-visiting ideas of 'community' and 'leadership' already encountered in discussions of the practice of a priest. This may remind us of a comment by Rainer Maria Rilke, *"and all the words they use are so worn."*

the practice of priesthood

However, the words encountered in this study – spirituality and authority as well as community and leadership – are worn by the respondents in daily use.

a number of challenges

It is generally recognised that the Roman Catholic Church faces a number of challenges to what it teaches with authority. These are frequently topics of conversation amongst laity and priests, despite attempts at ruling out discussion as pointless in the face of authoritative decision on the very possibility of change or a more complex ignoring of the issues. Chapter Six examines the views of respondents on a selection of controversial issues: celibacy, offering communion to Christians of other denominations, women priests, artificial contraception, the validity of Anglican orders, married priests, and sacramental participation of the divorced and re-married.

Chapter Seven attempts to look at the responses of participants in the round rather than as particular answers to specific questions. It suggests a typology of orientations that moves beyond a simple distinction between 'left' and 'right', and 'traditional' and 'liberal'. Combining notions of priest and of Church, it outlines three sets of attitudes: sacred priest – closed Church; priests as functionaries in an organisational Church; communitarian priest – open Church.

Chapter Eight and Nine present theological reflections on the study. First, Kenneth Wilson, a Methodist minister and theologian places the work as part of the self-understanding of the Church in a God-made world. Second, Paul Conroy, a parish priest with experience of seminary teaching, explores the inevitability of the tensions and differences illustrated in this study. Taken together these two chapters illustrate the conviction of the Working Party that there should be inter-play between theological reflection and empirical enquiry.

the actual words of respondents

Throughout the text and in the title the actual words of respondents have been presented so that the reader is enabled to appreciate the experiences and the beliefs of this group of bishops, priests, seminarians, and those no longer in ministry. Their words are, of course, not attributable, and where priests are named their comments derive from a recent collection 'Faith, Hope and

Chastity: Honest Reflections from the Catholic Priesthood' (ed. Butler, 1999). For similarly illustrative purposes Appendix Two contains selected findings from the 1993 survey of Catholic priests in America on attitudes to ecclesiological and theological issues, and problems facing priests (Hoge, Shields and Griffin).

The author is indebted to the interviewers and those they interviewed in the NOP survey. He also wishes to express gratitude to the Queen's Working Party, and in particular to Dr. David Barker and the Rev. Dr. Kenneth Wilson for commenting on an earlier draft.

Chapter One

THE PRACTICE OF PRIESTHOOD

THIS CHAPTER CONSIDERS two of the structural elements in the practice of priesthood in the Roman Catholic Church: priesthood as service, and the varying ecclesial models in which and to which service is offered.

Priesthood as service

> *"the **essence** of priesthood is to be of service. It is not about status."* (Fr. McTernan in ed. Butler 1999 p.57)

'Service' is a word used by respondents across the categories in answer to a question about the meaning of priesthood.

> *"I see myself as being a priest to carry out a certain ministry, which is another way of saying to carry out a work of service for the people in a very specific way."* (Bishop)

> *"The first word that comes to mind is service. At the end of the day, I have to be a priest to the people, to serve the way Christ served. It does not mean authority or prestige or power. It means working and living alongside people, sharing in their joys and sorrows in the name of Christ."* (Recently ordained)

> *"Priesthood means a call by God to serve the community. It is a full-time, active role."* (Resigned)

> *"Priesthood is giving a specialised service to others, in the sense that you can celebrate the sacraments, you can be with people at their high and low points, and as a general sort of work you can help them as well in various ways."* (Non-parochial)

> *"The first thing that comes to mind is priest and parish at Sunday Mass. But it is a far bigger role than that. It is a life of service to God and to the people by administering and preparing them for the sacraments, developing their faith, counselling and being there when they want you."* (Seminarian)

> *"Priesthood is primarily the service of the people of God."*
> (Parish priest)

> *"I have no expectations other than being able to serve people and help them in their faith."* (Seminarian)

Whilst the same word 'service' is used in each of these extracts, it appears that different conceptions are at work. If we ask who is the primary object of service related to what seems to be a general priestly office of leadership, we can begin to unpack 'service' as part of the rhetoric of contemporary Roman Catholic priesthood. In doing so we frequently meet issues of status.

Priesthood can be seen in primary and in secondary terms. It can be primarily a service directed to the deity and to self-development in a personal relationship with Christ.

> *"Priesthood is a calling, being chosen for service, primarily of Christ, but then of the people of whom you are given pastoral care."* (Non-parochial)

The implicit status difference involved in being chosen for service of Christ and being given people for pastoral care is denied by a seminarian who nonetheless sees the work of a priest as essentially directed towards God.

> *"The meaning of priesthood is a very difficult question. It means a lot to me... To me it's not a special role. It's no better nor worse than for a normal Christian. It's essentially giving my life to God. For me that is what priesthood is about, and hopefully to bring God to those around you."* (Seminarian)

> *"Priesthood has essentially something to do with the relationship you have with God which has its ups and downs, but has always gone on within the Catholic Church... Priesthood involves the constant development of your being as conforming yourself to be like Christ."* (Seminarian)

Status considerations are more clearly involved when we consider the content of a priest's service. For some the special *"conforming to be like Christ"* constitutes the service they offer: they

> *"represent Christ to the community. We administer sacraments to the faithful and preach the word of God. It is a sacramental and a sacrificial priesthood... We represent Christ at the altar."*
>
> (Non-parochial)

> *"The priest is called to be an icon of Christ. Through the grace of ordination, Christ shows himself through you and your ministry."* (Recently ordained)

> *"The first thing I think of is the sacraments, saying mass and so on. This is an external expression of the fact that people want God and we give people God in the seven sacraments. Everything in life from the day you are born is related to the Church through the priests. I'm old fashioned enough to think it is the priest rather than everybody together. I think of the ministry of the priesthood and not the ministry of the laity."*
>
> (Parish priest)

The source of these elevated notions of priesthood in the ontological change of status conveyed at ordination will be considered in Chapter Three when we look at routes to the practice of priesthood. At this stage we could usefully note that ideas of the priest as serving as a kind of God-conduit have been criticised by those outside and those inside the present study. Father Inch, for example, believes that priesthood is *"not about piously bringing God into people's lives. It is about helping people recognise the presence of God already in their lives and bringing people to celebrate"* (ed. Butler 1999, p.99). A priest in the sample we are considering no longer in official ministry concluded:

> *"that we are moving in the Catholic Church away from an understanding of the priesthood... where the priest was seen to be the holy man, based on Old Testament categories, ... and dealing with the sacraments... My own understanding and I think that of many people in the Church now is that the priesthood is more Christ with the people, and we are there to sanctify the world with the people, so there is a function of leadership, of teaching the word, of presiding at the Eucharistic function and so on, but the sacramentality of it is giving way to a better understanding of the fact that the Church is people... Part of the tension in the Church as present is that*

priest was seen to be the holy man

the leadership to a great extent has not really understood this revolution in thinking... for example for many years now I have not worn what is considered traditional dress for clergy, simply because I feel it would put me at a distance from other people. (Resigned)

The content of priestly service may also be seen primarily as pastoral in nature.

"Priesthood for me is very much linked to the idea of service. It's hard to know because priesthood is such a big concept... The pastoral side is very meaningful to me. I think it's about sharing people's lives really, being with them in good times and in different times and just sort of trying to represent Christ and help people, to act as a sort of facilitator, and make oneself available to other people and their needs." (Seminarian)

So extensive an availability to unmet need is capable of generating a one-sided response.

"At happy times, marriage and baptism, people are dependent on you, and I found that to be great." (Resigned)

This one-sided response is also evident in the view that the specific service of the priest is to exercise leadership:

"A priest is somebody who is specifically set aside and called by God to do a particular task of leading a group of Christians within the community, celebrating the sacraments for them and caring for them pastorally." (Recently ordained)

"I would now see the priest as someone who is called to be a leader of his people, to draw out of them their talents and abilities and to encourage and empower them to work as true disciples of Christ." (Bishop)

There are, of course, different styles of leadership. One respondent no longer in active ministry described the change in his approach following Vatican II.

"I became more democratic, hoping people would regard me as chairman of the meeting rather than the priest who did all the

> *people are dependent on you*

work, who was remote, who did a mystical job. I hoped that my priesthood would be as a brother to the people."

It is perhaps recognition of status considerations involved in talking of leadership that leads one seminarian to a notion of 'humble' leadership and to doubts expressed by another respondent:

"The priest is in one sense a leader, but in another he should not be." (Non-parochial)

The idea of leadership as dependent on the kind of task in hand rather than dependent on office is clearly voiced by the parish priest who commented:

"I might be the leader in certain areas, but not in all... Nowadays, people in the parishes should play their rightful role."

Questions concerning the different areas in which leadership is called for will be considered later.

In what kind of Church do priests locate their work?

A question concerning the model of church adopted by respondents encountered some interesting difficulties. This is not surprising when a term primarily of analysis is treated as if it was a term of art. As Lonergan (1972) has stated, models are *"not descriptions of reality, not hypotheses about reality, but simply interlocking sets of terms and relations"* (p. 284). Seminarians were familiar with thinking in terms of models, but some serving priests had difficulties with the concept. *"I am not used to being questioned in this way. The Church is like a big happy family with the bishops as father."* (Parish priest), but some married respondents reflecting on their experience of family life pointed out that the family can act as an important sounding board and that certain kinds of control are incompatible with family life.

"You tend not to think too deeply about these in the midst of things. A modern vision is to deepen Christian life. I wouldn't sacrifice that for a sense of the holy in the Church." (Parish priest)

The Church is like a big happy family

> *"I haven't thought of it in terms of models. The Church is a divine society, a body founded by God to communicate salvation to the human race."* (Parish priest)

Others, though more familiar with the notion of models of church, found that:

the community aspect

> *"None appeals much. The pilgrim church is a nice phrase but it is not always clear what it means. The community aspect is important. Body of Christ? I haven't found bishops any better than the Pope."* (Non-parochial)

For some a plurality of models is to be welcomed.

> *"When I started out in formation, my model was very institutional. I still value the Church as an institution very much, but I now hold several models at the same time. The Church is also prophet, and if it is not marginalised it cannot do its job properly. The Church is a sacrament, a sign of the presence of God, pointing to a Kingdom which is not the world's way of doing things."* (Non-parochial)

Those who felt constrained to choose one model either coupled the hierarchical with the charismatic or the view of the Church as **communio**, or emphasised one particular orientation.

the Church is hierarchical and charismatic

> *"The Church is hierarchical and charismatic. Hierarchical in that it has a structure with Christ as its head. Charismatic in that the Holy Spirit is at the centre."* (Newly ordained)

> *"I see Church as communion, the people of God gathered, beyond time and space. It is not bound by locality. I understand the hierarchical nature of the church, not in opposition to communion. You can't have communion without the hierarchy serving it. You can't have hierarchy unless you have communion. The Church is the people of God hierarchically gathered."* (Newly ordained)

Others chose one model emphasising pilgrim/pilgrimage; collaboration; mystical body of hierarchical ordering in a simple form or community.

The ideas of a pilgrim Church and a Church on pilgrimage both contain the notion of a journey, but going on a pilgrimage involves direction and continuous movement towards a specified destination.

> *"I would see the Church as being best compared to a pilgrimage, and by that I mean a group of people bonded together by a common purpose and a love of each other. Direction and leadership is important, probably by priests and bishops, but not exclusively. People are not expected to be marching in time and all at the same pace. There are also people who find it difficult, and people who drop off."* (Bishop)

Those who rely more on a notion of pilgrim are less certain of the route and are not always able to specify the destination for a bonded group.

> *"The Church is like a Sherpa guide who is there to make sure you get to the top of the mountain, not to get to the top for you. I see the Church as an aide to get the people where God wants them to be; to seize and fulfil their own personal ministry."* (Seminarian)

> *"We have a sense of where we are going and we know we are on the way and that everybody on the journey is important. We do not know the details of the route, and although there is an end in sight, sometimes it is obscured. Only by faith do we know where we are going."* (Bishop)

we have a sense of where we are going

A variety of responses appear to be variants on the theme of collaboration; for instance, community or fellowship, the people of God, and the collegial or open models. In all these cases, the role of the individual ministries of all the members of Church is considered to be of particular importance. Participants found it relatively easy to explain, though in very general terms, how these collaborative models could be put into practice.

> *"My model of the Church is essentially a community with Christ at the centre, where everybody has an irreplaceable contribution to make... It is made up of concrete localities across the world, each adapted to local circumstances and conditions, but there is a common faith uniting everybody."*
> (Bishop)

> *"My model follows the teaching of the Church. Vatican II proposed a model that was collegial and inclusive and open while retaining all the essentials of being the Church. There is a role for all people in the Church. I would go for this rather than the command system."* (Parish priest)

> *"It is a community or fellowship... All the people are called to a relationship with God and each other based on love."*
> (Non-parochial)

> *"The Church is a community. It's everybody together, sharing the love of God. To an extent the Church is a pyramid with the Pope on top, but the true Church is every believing Christian. This is what makes it difficult to implement the model because you are asking people to realise their relationship with other people. Basically you are asking people to have a change of heart. Human nature as it is today is out for 'what I can get.' People will not listen and that gets you down sometimes."* (Seminarian)

> *"My model of the Church is collaborative ministry. It means honest dialogue at all times. When I first came here, we voted to change the times of the Mass."* (Parish priest)

'Community' figures in many of the responses

"Community" figures in many of the responses we have been studying. It also figures in almost every discussion of the contemporary Church. As Hornsby-Smith (1989) has noted. "There are few words more highly regarded among Catholics than "Community." (p. 66) The present study suggests that the word is used in accordance with distinguishable conceptions; common usage conceals different uses. So "community' is used simply as another name for the local society:

> *"Ministry also extends to anyone in the community, not just the Church, who wants your ministry. You try and take the Christian message of hope, faith and love out into the community. You do that in conjunction with other Christians."*
> (Resigned)

"Community" is also used in relation to groupings of varying size and inter-connection. Some respondents advocate breaking down the parish community into much smaller communities, and see people coming to church as a community to share their experiences of life. This presumably entails that those regularly attending the same mass constitute a community. Communities can also be envisaged as capable of action and themselves as also the subject of action of a specific kind. So, communities are seen as granting forgiveness, exercising authority, choosing ministers. They can also feature as the result of a minister building-up and fostering community. Those criticising seminary education find that enclosed community living is no preparation for life in *"the community"*. Talk of community, where it occurs in a religious context, has, as Lonergan (1972) argues, to discern and distinguish a common field of experience, common or complementary ways of understanding, common judgements and common values, goals and policies.

talk of community

In general, those priests who were no longer in active ministry were more sceptical about the extent to which their ideal for the Church existed in reality, though their models tended to be community-based, or to focus on democratic ideas. Several commented that they felt the Church should not be modelled as a dictatorship, pyramid or hierarchy. They advocated models such as concentric circles, a network of communities, and a wheel.

> *"A community structure is a circle of God within it, not a triangle… With the circular model, change will come from below, by raising and discussing issues.* (Resigned)

> *"Since Vatican II, the old model of the pyramid is still prevalent … My model is a wheel where the rim is the most important part: the people of God. The hub at the centre is the teaching of the Gospel. The spokes take the power of that to the rim; those spokes would be priests, who are there to support and sustain.* (Resigned)

The models so far illustrated have in common an understanding of Church in terms of other social arrangements. We already possess a sufficient idea of journey, pilgrimage, collaboration and so on. Such an approach is emphatically rejected by those who see the Church as a mystical body or as a mystery.

> *"My model is not significant. The only model that matters is

> *that of Jesus Christ. There is no one model. The Church is a servant, is hierarchical, everything. Each has an element of truth. The Church is essentially a mystery. It is not like Kelloggs Cornflakes or IBM. The Church is a mystery presenting us Jesus Christ. I can never get a model for the Church which is even vaguely adequate because the Church is the body of Christ."* (Parish priest)

> *"The Church is not simply a human institution, it is a divine entity… with Christ at its head and the other baptised forming the body."* (Recently ordained)

a mystery is not a problem to be solved

Thinking of the Church as a divine entity or a mystery may seem to bring conversation to a halt but this need not be the case. Obviously a mystery is not a problem to be solved but as Lonergan (1972) has argued, *"the ongoing contexts within which mystery is adored and adoration is explained are anything but free from problems. Least of all at the present time is the existence of problems to be ignored. For now problems are so numerous that many do not know what to believe. They are not unwilling to believe. They know what church doctrines are. But they want to know what church doctrines could possibly mean."* (p. 345)

Conclusion

It is clear that in descriptions of the practice of priesthood 'service' struggles with status: it is difficult to sustain ideas of 'separate but not superior' if a priest is viewed as called by God in some special way. 'Service' itself, as we have seen, can be used in the context of different conceptions. It is not the simple notion it first appears to be. What, for example, distinguishes the service offered or rendered by the priest from the service to which all Christians are called? Some of the problems raised by this question can be glimpsed in the comment by a non-parochial priest:

> *"The priest is there as the servant of everybody else. You could say we are all called to serve — everything in the Gospel is about service — but, the priest is there to facilitate others in their lives. The authority of the priest is the authority of the servant, but this only makes sense with the Gospel."*

In the light of the Gospel one could also ask who offers service to priests?

Priests picture the Church in a variety of ways some of which suggest already extant achievement, as in the idea of Church as a divinely founded means of the communication of salvation or as a big happy family, and others which indicate a notion of journeying towards a varyingly specific goal with more or less confidence. Some see a plurality of models as a sign of institutional health. Others seek to combine two models or to see the possibility of only one dominant picture. The notion of communio now receives considerable emphasis, but like 'community' on which it is parasitic, at least in part, it is capable of more than one interpretation. Plant (1974) has pointed to conservative and to liberal views of 'community'. Similarly, 'communio' can be used to emphasise equality of membership or the distinctive and essential role of a central authority.

The discussion of 'models' by respondents indicates the importance of recognising the distinct use of metaphor. What should be avoided is the move without perplexity from metaphor to substantive conclusion about Church governance and priestly authority. So, a view of Church as family could lead to an unsatisfactory search for the father, presumably the mother and so on. Another example of the unjustified use of metaphor comes from outside the present sample. Cardinal Francis George in a discussion of episcopal conferences (1999) moves from *"the Church as the Body of Christ"* to the conclusion *that "just as monstrous as a head without a body is a body without a head."* Metaphorical bodies simply **do** not operate in this manner. If they do, they are not metaphorical.

Ideas of a serving Church and a priesthood of service can be taken forward in two ways. First, Church and priesthood can be re-located in the extensive literature on altruism. For example, the European Values Study has attempted to distinguish between the possible reasons for work on behalf of others: as an expression of solidarity with the poor and disadvantaged, as compassion, a sense of duty, to bring about social and political change, and so on. (Timms, 1992; Ashford and Timms, 1992) Second, we should explore those notions (of status, power over, and so on) against which 'service' is used as a counter-balance. Does 'service' come into its own through what, so to speak, it chases out? Some of the complexities involved have been captured in Terry Eagleton's novel, Saints and Scholars. Here it is said that the Dominican Prior, Father Gore-Knox *"had revolted against his patrician background, abandoning a career of ordering people around for a lifetime of service to their needs. He did not realise that the latter was simply a more subtle version of the former".*

Chapter Two

ORIENTATION TO THE PRACTICE OF A PRIEST

THIS CHAPTER BEGINS by reporting on the actual objectives of priesthood, on the kinds of future priests are attempting to realise. It then considers some of the attitudes priests bring to their work, enquiring specifically whether in the light of the problems they perceive within the Church and within current society, they are optimistic or pessimistic. This provides one important indication of the state of clergy morale. This chapter ends by examining the value respondents place on some of the second-order notions – in comparison to the first order orientations of service and of Church already discussed – available for making their work intelligible to themselves and others. These second-order notions or particular applications concern the priest as manager, as professional, as a person in need both of career development and of appraisal whether through systematic evaluation or feedback from parishioners.

Working objectives

It is perhaps to be expected that seminarians envisage objectives that are both very general and very demanding. As one said,

> "I am open-minded, having known a number of priests over the years... To be first and foremost someone who tries to live out the philosophy of life based in Scripture and to share that with other people."

However, ordained priests also tend to set objectives in terms which make difficult any assessment of any approximation in achieving them. The exception to this was the parish priest whose principal priority was to increase the numbers coming to mass. The remainder express much more general objectives which seem to divide into those pertaining to the parish and those pointing beyond. Examples of the former include:

> "I want to break down barriers between myself and others."
>
> (Non-parochial)

seminarians envisage objectives that are both very general and very demanding

> *"I am trying to make the parish self-reliant, with a life of its own."* (Parish priest)
>
> *"I would like to build up a community of real believers."*
> (Parish priest)

Those pointing to a world beyond the parish think primarily in terms of justice and peace:

> *"I would like a future where young people would have principles in life: honesty, integrity, charity and justice. In the long run that is the key to happiness."* (Parish priest)
>
> *"Primarily, it is bringing the word of God to the people and showing them the idea of social justice."*

However, the world of 'objectives' and a realisable future can be uncertain. Respondents can attempt to realise objectives that address 'churchy' concerns and those of the wider world.

> *"You are trying to help people get to heaven and to make Christianity fit into their lives… and to make the parish open and adaptable to the needs of the community."* (Parish priest)
>
> *"I want a future that is going back to moral standards and commitment to the Church, and a more equal distribution of resources."* (Seminarian)

Problems and opportunities facing the Church

Any practice assumes both a supportive and a conflicted internal environment, and a wider world with which the practice is engaged. In this study respondents were asked about the main problems and opportunities facing the Roman Catholic Church, and whether they were optimistic about the future.

The practice of priesthood is carried on in an unsettled internal environment. Lack of vocations and falling numbers caused general concern.

> *"There is a desperate shortage of priests compared to what we are used to… The most demanding and difficult job I have is appointing clergy, because you often have to tell communities to*

share a priest... and there will always be some square pegs in round holes." (Bishop)

This naturally leads to an insistent question:

"Why aren't people coming forward as ministers and leaders in the Church, particularly as priests and religious?" (Resigned)

The problem of attracting young people to membership was another 'recruitment' issue at the forefront of respondents' minds. A number reported that the Church is now suffering the effect of a loss of faith in the past two generations, describing these as *"the lost generations"*. Thus, many children are growing up in families with little Christian influence, and a large proportion of the adult population has little or no understanding of the Christian faith.

"We have lost a generation of young adults... around the early 1970's... Those people were kids then and are parents now. They are sending kids to Catholic school, but they don't know why... They feel they ought to. One challenge is to grasp the fact that catechetical work needs to be done with adults as with children. (Bishop)

"We seem to have lost two generations in a huge area of Europe." (Seminarian)

A partial explanation for such a loss is to be found in the exercise of Church authority, but from two conflicting perceptions. On the one hand respondents complain of a loss of nerve and a failure to exercise authority. On the other hand the complaint is of a faulty model of authority.

"People do not understand their faith these days... The bishops have not given much lead on this. You mention things and they do not want to discuss them... There is something wrong with us, but if you say that to people in authority, they just don't want to know... Authority does not want to be disturbed. They don't want to face up to questions people ask, but they have to, now or in the future." (Non-parochial)

"The major issue is how the Church can bring God's message to the people in a constantly changing society. Once we

> *a loss of nerve and a failure to exercise authority*

> *establish where we are going then we can start to answer the other issues such as celibacy, married priests and women priests."* (Seminarian)
>
> *"Within the Church, there is an individualistic approach; people pick and choose those aspects of the Church which appeal to them and disregard the others... You will find it among the clergy too... People make themselves the arbiter, and conform the truth to their own predispositions."* (Parish priest)
>
> *"There are people in the Church who challenge authority per se... It brings disharmony. They talk about the official Church and get angry, and they don't realise they are all officially in the Church."* (Recently ordained)

Those no longer in active ministry tended to be more outspoken about concerns over authority.

> *"I am not impressed by Church authorities and what they are doing... The Church is not in touch with the young; it is an ageing priesthood."* (Resigned)
>
> *"The Pope... has placed in positions of power all over the world conservative or acquiescent people. That is a major problem for the Church. Much of the leadership is timid because of this authority model they have."* (Resigned)
>
> *"The main problem is that, having been given the vision of renewal by Vatican II, the Church hierarchy have had cold feet. So you have the current of the Council carrying people in one direction, and the cross-current of the restoration of the pre-Vatican II status quo imposed by the Vatican."* (Resigned)

people were perceived to be unreceptive to any authority

The wider society in which the Church has a place was also pictured as in a critical condition. Individualism and materialism were believed to have resulted in a *"selfish"* society in which Gospel values were no longer esteemed or even thought applicable by the majority of the population, and moral relativism holds sway. A few participants went as far as to describe the current atmosphere in society as *"pagan"*. This poses a problem for Church authority because people were perceived to be unreceptive to *any* authority claiming moral jurisdiction.

> *"One serious problem now is secularisation: individual self-centredness along with a loss of the idea of God... It goes clean against Gospel values."* (Bishop)

> *"We are in a world that is quite pagan and dotty... which seems to have lost all contact with truth and reality."* (Bishop)

> *"The Church is concerned with faith, doctrines and morals, but people don't like being told what is right and wrong now."*
> (Non-parochial)

Additionally, media representation of the Church was thought to be one-sided and misleading, stereotyping the Church and damaging its efforts to establish relationships within the wider community. Church scandals were thought to receive excessive media attention.

> *"The media seems to misrepresent us. We are a laughing stock in our country. The general image is the Father Ted image."*
> (Seminarian)

Optimism or pessimism about the future

The responses fall into three groupings: those denying either attitude, those broadly optimistic, and those expressing a qualified pessimism.

Some consciously avoided optimism or pessimism, and simply relied on faith, in order to set about trying to achieve what they could in their own ministry.

> *"I am neither optimistic nor pessimistic. You just have to do the best you can in the circumstances... You have to put your trust in God and keep going."* (Parish priest)

> *"It is a question of faith. It is up to the Holy Spirit to reveal to me what the Holy Spirit wants."* (Parish priest)

> *"I'm neither. Optimism and pessimism have nothing to do with Christianity. I'm hopeful although I can see that we will continue to have falling numbers of priests and people coming to Church."* (Bishop)

simple reliance on faith

A number of participants commented that optimism was obligatory because the future is in God's hands. Given the limitations of human understanding and foresight, some participants simply accept that the Holy Spirit will work through the Church, providing guidance and inspiration for the unforeseeable future. Others rely on their faith to maintain their optimism.

> "As a Christian, I have to be optimistic. Hope is a virtue we neglect too often. In today's society, with decreasing numbers and so on, it can be quite difficult to be people of hope. But, please God, I have enough faith and hope to be optimistic."
>
> (Bishop)

> "Personally and theologically, I think the Church will always be optimistic because Christ is triumphant and we share in that… The future is in God's hands. We have such a limited vision." (Recently ordained)

> "We have to be optimistic. The Holy Spirit works in the Church." (Non-parochial)

> "Ultimately I am optimistic about the future of the Church because as Catholics we believe that Christ made the promise to the Church that He would be with her until the end of time." (Parish priest)

active optimism about the future

The majority of serving priests and seminarians express active optimism about the future. Reasons for this include the essential goodness of people, the relevance of Christianity, and a faith that God will keep the Church alive. Additionally, some felt that despite an apparent loss of numbers and interest in the Church, history and the Gospel suggest that pessimism is inappropriate. These participants perceived or expected a resurgence of faith and described the Church as *"vital"* and *"developing"*.

> "I am optimistic in the sense that I am sure it is going to come right and there will be a great revival." (Bishop)

> "I am optimistic. I believe the Gospel is always going to have a value in society." (Non-parochial)

> "I am optimistic. I see good things happening and good people around me." (Parish priest)

> *"I am optimistic... When the Church seems to be dying, that is the prelude to a resurrection."* (Parish priest)
>
> *"I am optimistic, despite the reduced numbers of clergy and people in the Church. It is an exciting place to be, it is changing and developing."* (Parish priest)
>
> *"As the younger generation grow up, I think there will be more openness to Christianity... it is the answer to the world's problems: a way of teaching true love."* (Parish priest)
>
> *"I am optimistic. I see signs of good things happening, which often go unnoticed."* (Seminarian)

Other participants were pessimistic about the future of the Church, given the problems it faces currently. However, several also argued that the survival of the Church through previous times of difficulty suggested that it would recover. Indeed, some pointed out that the Gospel explains that the Church will face persecution but will nevertheless survive and triumph.

The Church will recover

> *"Sometimes I am pessimistic when I look at numbers; young people are falling away. Yet when you look at the Church over 2000 years, this period is not peculiar. When they write the history of this period, I think they will say what a great time it was to be alive; the Church was vital, not static."* (Parish priest)
>
> *"I am pessimistic thinking that humans are frail, but that makes us need one another and a saviour, and so I am hopeful. My wider view is to look at 2000 years of history... There were problems in Paul's time, so there will be today and tomorrow."*
> (Seminarian)
>
> *"I am a bit pessimistic because I can see society moving away from the Church, and the Church cannot follow because she has principles to stand up for."* (Seminarian)

Interestingly, those priests who had resigned their active ministry were also broadly optimistic about the future. Nonetheless they often criticised the institution of the Church at present, and looked forward to the possibility of change in the future.

> *"I am always an optimist... but I fear the Catholic Church as an institution will suffer more rough rides before it reforms."*
> (Resigned)

27

"I'm pessimistic in the present situation because Rome refuses to discuss certain issues such as the ordination of women... but I am also optimistic because the crisis in number of priests is reaching political importance... The Church will have to face it." (Resigned)

"About the long term future, I am optimistic. The Second Vatican Council made all the preparations for a missionary Church." (Resigned)

"I would claim to be extremely optimistic. At a superficial level, the Church is rent in two because two parties formed at the time of the Second Vatican Council, polarised and have not agreed an accommodation in thirty years... The reality has gone out of the old structure of the Vatican... It does not understand sex, liberty or intellectual conscientious freedom... If you discount that, the field is open to an immense amount of creativity and experimentation." (Resigned)

Chapter three notes the connection Emmet (1972) has made between vocation and creativity.

Second-order notions

In view of the demanding and general nature of the objectives of the priesthood and of the persistence for most of attitudes of optimism, do priests find any value in second-order notions in the ordering and assessment of their day-to-day work? Potentially, a number are available: parish manager, professional person, servant of the bishop, servant of the parish, minister to a sacramental routine, pursuing opportunities, solving problems. A few respondents would reject the idea that any of these can provide even a foothold in the ascent to making the life of a priest intelligible and accountable. Only another priest can understand the life of his fellow.

Priests as parish managers

Priest as manager of the parish

Some simply rejected the connotations of the term manager applied to priests.

"The term does not make any sense to me. A manager is someone in industry or someone who runs a bank. I would not see parents as the 'managers' of the family. It does not express the role of service." (Recently ordained)

> *"I'm very uncomfortable with the word manager because of the images associated – largely administrative which is not the deeper significance of priesthood. It certainly has something to do with leadership, though some may see 'leader' as a pejorative term. Leadership has to be exercised as Christ would have envisaged it. The model of friendship is better than manager, an openness to lead by example and to lead in the midst."*
>
> (Seminarian)

Friendship, as we will see was not an experience many of the older priests associated with seminary life.

> *"The most important thing I do every day is celebrate mass and this is the primary way you help people towards a relationship with God."* (Non-parochial)

Others recognise the notion of management but express personal antipathy or ambivalence.

> *"I don't do any more managing that I have to. I keep my hand in in relation to finance because that is necessary because I am answerable. I oversee things, that's all. Spread out the control."*
>
> (Non-parochial)

> *"I do see myself as parish manager and it frightens me, because it's the one thing I'm not good at."*

> *"It's not a role I relish. Before you know where you are you're running a plant, almost secular in the demands it makes upon you. You are forced into a managerial role but I would much prefer to be a spiritual leader, but it's very difficult to get voluntary lay assistance, for example on the material fabric."*
>
> (Parish priest)

The apparent relish expressed half-jokingly by the parish priest who compared his role in parish affairs to that of a benevolent Pinochet is not generally shared, but a robust acceptance of a management role is evident in some responses.

a benevolent Pinochet

> *"On the negative side nothing must happen that I don't know."* (Parish priest)

> *"The priest has to be in control of everything that is going on in the parish. The more he can get people to collaborate in the*

life of the Church the better. Some things cannot be delegated – to do with the eucharistic ministry and preaching." (Recently ordained)

"Practically we are managers in the sense that we manage resources and buildings and are called to be leaders in the Church. We have to manage people, to initiate, encourage and organise." (Recently ordained)

"I go along with things for a year and then introduce change. You could call it a subtle kind of manipulation… I wait before I challenge. I'm there for them. If I turn them against me I've lost my opportunity. It's a very difficult tightrope to walk. I don't cave in to everything." (Non-parochial)

ministry as functional

Further light is shed on the practice of priesthood by considering responses to a question concerning the extent to which respondents saw their ministry as functional. Functional, of course, has many meanings, and as one parish priest acknowledged,

" 'Functional' is not in my vocabulary… if the rain is coming in the grace of God won't stop it."

No respondent referred to the wide societal functions priesthood might perform. For example, in relation to the Anglican priesthood Mason (1992) has argued that:

"Priesthood then has to do for all society what various individuals do for others within it, that is, maintain moral security in the face of the threat of dissolution… It represents the whole of a society to its members, gathering up in its traditions all that society finds most significant. From another point of view it has to cut loose from society and show that those things which are most to be valued among men and women are not their own but the gift of God." (p. 11)

Only one respondent in the present study approached this way of interpreting function when he referred to the priest as functional for people.

"It depends on the meaning of 'functional'. If people see you as a person who can function in their lives, then, it is. If they

> don't see you as any use at all, then, for them it's not functional. If you say mass and people are there you are being a function for them. A lot of priestly function is done by lay people." (Non-parochial)

The reference to the Eucharist is echoed by those who think in terms of sacramental functions.

> "The priesthood is functional. A priest is the servant of the Church, and in any organism certain functions have to be carried out, if you call preaching and sacramental celebration a function... The Church was given the divine function to baptise and to spread the word." (Parish priest)

> "I hope it is not all functional, in the sense of just jobs and tasks. The person that you are is very important. I try not to be anybody else. I try to be myself, but there are functions that have to be performed. You have to celebrate mass, have to baptise." (Parish priest)

> "To a large extent it is functional. You often don't feel like going to church and you have to be there every day. There's a lot of function in the set offices." (Recently ordained)

A number of respondents express concern that 'function' in the sense of carrying out sacramental functions and in the sense of administration can act as a hindrance to ministry.

> "The priest's job is becoming more functional; it's a small business really... It gets in the way of pastoral work. It's functional in relation to the sacraments. The elderly expect mass every day. You do become a mass machine; it becomes very functional." (Recently ordained)

> "We have a responsibility for maintenance but I don't think the ministry is for just parish maintenance. Ministry can be hindered because of the other things the priest has to do."
> (Seminarian)

> "Administration stops you from doing what you could be doing. For example, parish visiting." (Seminarian)

> "You could spend a lot of time on administration. You have to

ministry can be hindered because of the other things a priest has to do

> be disciplined to say, I've done enough administration today, I'm off visiting." (Recently ordained)
>
> "A lot of the present work is functional. I say to candidates we are often very good at doing priesthood, cramming lots into the day, and this chimes in with the moves of society. Being a priest has to be rediscovered. In my life you can easily get caught up in the 'doing' contrasted with the 'being'." (Non-parochial)

This emphasis on **being** priestly is supported by a recently ordained priest, but he believes that the functional can be integrated into or disappear within the main purpose of priesthood.

> "The ministry is not solely functional. The functional things assist the primary purpose. All the functional things could go. There are lots of different ways in which one can exercise the priesthood: it is a way of being."

Priest as a professional

Another possible way of ordering a practice is to conceive it as falling within those occupations that are accepted as professional. This possibility is raised in relation to parish priests by Hornsby-Smith (1989) precisely in consideration of *"what it is that they are specialised in or committed to. And there is a great deal of evidence worldwide that for many priests the answer has not been very clear... In the first place there is a lack of consensus in the literature about the extent to which the clergy can be considered to be a professional occupation"* (p. 126) The present study reports on the views of priests, particularly in relation to current interest in clergy appraisal. (See report in the Tablet, May 8th, 1989).

against a 'professional' model

Participants were generally against the idea of the priest following a 'professional' model. The ideal was to follow the role of Jesus Christ. A worldly model would not be fitting. Many also felt that to work within the sphere of a professional role model was too restricting – the priest must be able to enter any type of situation, even of a very personal and/or emotional nature. To have to act as a 'professional' would cross certain necessary boundaries: in effect the priest would not be able to do his job properly.

> "There is but one model and that's the Lord. I don't need any other model." (Recently ordained)

> *"The priesthood is different to other 'professions'. I suppose we are a profession but our profession is to serve, Christ is our role [model] and we are working in His name. We serve the needs of the people."* (Parish priest)

> *"It's a ludicrous idea: no income, no perks. There's damn all in the job for God's sake."* (Parish priest)

Others question the social implications of any successful claim to professional status.

> *"I'm totally against [a professional model] because it disqualifies people who aren't professionals and disempowers them from taking part. Professionalising the clergy has been a disaster and should be stopped."* (Resigned)

> *"Sometimes you might imagine yourself a professional talking to other professionals, and then you are on a council estate. You should feel a priest with both"* (Recently ordained)

And part of the way of life that constitutes priesthood involves rejecting the safeguards built into professionalism.

> *"The professional model is not right. To a degree we are professionals but not like any other professional. You can't cut off. It's a way of life. It's the scrutiny you're continually under. It's more of bearing witness to something. It's a 24 hour occupation. You have no rest from being a priest."* (Seminarian)

> *"I am a priest 24 hours a day – no profession could cope with that model. I'm wary of fitting into pre-fabricated structures, but we need more professionalism. Teachers have to cope with these models."* (Parish priest)

These last two statements indicate the very limited extent to which some elements of professional identity and of professionalism in behaviour may be admitted into conceptions of priesthood. It is interesting to note one of the trends reported in the 1993 American survey of priests: *"Priests in 1993 feel more akin to professional men like doctors, lawyers and educators than they did in 1970."* (Hoge, Shields and Griffin, 1993 p.25)

career had little appeal

The concept of career had little appeal. It was considered out of place in an occupation described as a vocation. This is partly because priests should not exercise control of their destiny.

> *"'Career' is not the spirit of priesthood. There are certain jobs I would love to do, but you have to respond to the situation you are put in. It's an aspect of religious life that you are put into situations you'd rather not. It's not for me to decide where I would be most effective."* (Seminarian)

> *"I'm unhappy with career development. I trust in the system. I make myself available."* (Recently ordained)

> *"I'm happy with my 'career', because I always do what the bishop tells me. This is an important part of my priesthood. It depends on his knowing his priests."* (Non-parochial)

> *"I have no control, and that's how I like it."* (Parish priest)

Another priest reported that his bishop had offered him a post he did not want. Two days later he visited the bishop and accepted the posting in a totally new field on the grounds that it was good to do what was difficult.

assessment and appraisal

Participants were more positive and more varied in their welcome to incorporating aspects of professional life into the role, such as assessment and appraisal. Over half the participants felt this would be a good way of receiving feedback on their progress, and would point up any problem areas, which had the potential to worsen.

> *"There is potential for a priest to become a little dictator over his church – this happens and with checks and balances, the reaction of the people in the parish, the opinions of bishops are important."* (Parish priest)

> *"Other people have got to go through appraisal in their work. It is important to check that we are doing the job we should be doing. We don't have any formal way to do that. It would be an affirmation if it went your way, that you are doing a good job even if numbers in the congregation are going down."*
> (Parish priest)

> *"We are looking at the whole question of appraisal, although I*

don't like the word very much because it has negative overtones ... I'm just instituting now a process where I will see individually each priest... it's an opportunity for me to explore with them where they're going and where they are... they've asked for that... more difficult would be the more technical appraisal." (Bishop)

Consideration of difficulties were certainly voiced by respondents.

"I'm against evaluation at parish level. It's the bishop's responsibility. It could become a sort of cronyism. Some form of consultation would be very useful, but no personality politics."
(Seminarian)

"Perhaps appraisal, but I'm so fed up after being in the seminary all that time, you just want to be left to be yourself... Personal lives should remain personal unless personal lives become a problem. They then become accountable. Accountability should only be in relation to your doing priestly things."
(Recently ordained)

"We need to practice humility, so no self-assessment." (Non-parochial)

"Appraisal will come, but who will appraise? Only a priest fully understands us. What happens if a priest does not pass or his workload has gone up because of a reduction in the number of priests? So we can't assess too much. Some of the younger priests are keen on assessment so that they can get more training. The bishop is assessing us all the time." (Parish priest)

"It's not easy to assess where you work in spiritual things."
(Retired)

Feedback from parishioners

If 'career', and 'profession' do only so much to make the practice of priesthood intelligible to priests, does meeting the wishes of the parish fare better? Some reject the notion in terms of the danger involved.

"It is dangerous to try to be all things to all people because you end up being nothing much to anybody." (Parish priest)

Others reject on more positive grounds:

> "I couldn't care a damn. I'm not here to be popular. It is the least of my concerns. For each person I meet I do what I am called to do." (Parish priest)

Another version of priestly work considers the serious consequences of not attending to the opinions of parishioners.

> "If you go against them [the parishioners] you won't continue to be a pilgrim church." (Seminarian)

> "At the parish level [lay involvement] is very important because people can vote with their feet... I want to take them with me. 99% of the time I want to make the decision that is most popular. There is no joy in a decision that is unpopular, because they won't be there to do it." (Parish priest)

Some suggest that the priest now has to work hard to overcome newly erected barriers.

> "Priesthood is no longer held in awe. There is not as much trust as there used to be. People demand more that they used. There is more questioning. Parishioners are more suspicious about what priesthood is and why people go into it. We would not necessarily go to a priest for the same issue. The whole perception of a priest has radically changed in the minds of people. Now the priest faces an automatic barrier which he has to break down by getting more involved in the community, and getting the community more involved in you. The priesthood is in crisis because of the sex scandals." (Seminarian)

At the same time, some priests felt they did not know what their parishioners really thought of them, and reported that feedback (either negative or positive) was often sadly lacking.

> "I would like to know more about how I am perceived by the parishioners. One does not always get a lot of feedback. It would be very helpful to know. I go out and visit, but people often don't make a direct comment about your own ministry."
> (Recently ordained)

> *"I have no idea; I hope they are happy with me... No one has complained about me to the bishop, that's the bottom line."*
>
> (Parish priest)

> *"Because we live a celibate lifestyle, without a spouse or somebody to point things out [the parish] is a good indication of whether we are doing things right or wrong."* (Parish priest)

However, deference can be positively valued.

> *"People behave differently around you; maybe that is a good thing; it reminds people of higher things."* (Seminarian)

Conclusion

This chapter raises a number of general questions. First, are the objectives of priest work to be bounded by consideration of parish or should they envisage a wider world? Fr. McTernan has put this question well: *"Having spent my whole ministry in two parishes, I finally believe in parish life. I think it would be a mistake to dismiss it; it's a very good way of living our Christian faith. But the limits of parish life have to be recognised. People's prime purpose in life is in the big wide world and the parish exists to help people live a more Christian life, whatever their condition or job."* (Butler, 1999, p.57)

the limits of parish life have to be recognised

Second, how well founded is the relative optimism of respondents in the face of problems within and outwith the Church? Is it based on 2000 years of Church history at a glance? Does it acknowledge sufficiently what, to use Wilde's turn of phrase, looks uncommonly like carelessness in the loss of two generations? If the Church can only respond by reiteration of teaching, then, it may have to embrace martyrdom. Such a possibility is outlined in the case of a particular Pope by Machiavelli.

> *"Although Pope Julius II during the period of filling the papal chair, acted with the greatest promptitude and violence, yet such conduct was agreeable to his times, and he prospered; but had they changed, and consequently moderation been rendered necessary, he would have certainly fallen a martyr to his principles, because he never would have complied."* (Bohn Standard Library, 1888, p.513)

Third, priests seem to struggle with ideas of the unique role of the priest. A professional model seems to question the total dedication to others: priesthood is not about management, though canonical responsibility should be acknowledged. Management, despite this, may run counter both to personal inclination and to the deeper significance of priesthood. In which case recruit the laity, but on whose terms?

Fourth, difficulties in the exercise of day-to-day ministry can be solved either through a simple acceptance of the idea of doing what the bishop requires or in some division between the priestly and 'other' aspects. The former position encounters the problem of change in management style discussed in Timms (ed. 2001). What happens when an ordinary very much in charge of an organisation is succeeded by one who seems to believe in putting responsibility on the individual priest? The latter is evident in the distinction between aspects of life that should be subject to appraisal and those that should not be.

Finally, the reference to friendship points to an important conceptualisation of the relationship between Christians, whether in authority or not, which avoids some of the problems of brotherhood and sisterhood. As Beiner (1983) has argued in a study of political judgement, *"Man **need** not be strangers; but from this it does not follow that they **can** be brothers. The concept of a friend is an intermediary between the two."* (p.122)

Chapter Three

ORDINATION: ROUTES AND OUTCOMES

THIS CHAPTER TRACES the paths by which priests come to find themselves in the role of servants in a particular kind of Church, and going about their work in a general spirit of optimism, though struggling through ideas of evaluation. It is divided into four main sections: reasons for becoming a priest, changes effected as a result of ordination, experiences of priestly formation at the seminary and beyond, and expectations of priesthood.

Reasons for becoming a priest

> *"It is a sacrament of vocation. Within the priesthood of all believers there are those set aside for the ordained priesthood."*
> (Recently ordained)

> *"A priest is somebody who is specifically set aside and called by God to do a particular task..."* (Recently ordained)

> *"I had a passionate conviction that God was calling me..."*
> (Resigned)

a sacrament of vocation

Only one priest, now no longer thinking of himself as a priest, described the experience of losing his vocation or, as he put it, his mother's.

The notion of vocation can best be understood, so Emmet (1972) has argued, both through a study of the specifically Christian context and also through broadening 'vocation' to refer primarily to *"creativeness within certain kinds of role"* (p.242)... *"We may consider under 'vocation' not only the great originality of innovation and pioneers, but also the creative resourcefulness of people who carry out already recognised social roles in a way of their own."* (p.244)

Within the Christian context Emmet notes the linking of the idea of vocation with the call to perfection. In the face of this linkage it is impossible to understand the musing of Colby in T.S. Eliot's

the call of God

'The Confidential Clerk'. One of the themes in this play is that of vocation in music, and Colby wonders if one can have a vocation to be a mediocre organist, like his father. Any call to perfection must present a problem for those who do not emphasise the idea of being set apart. The idea of responding to the call of God to do his will raises the conceptual problem of what it means to talk of the will of God and the pragmatic problem of identifying this will in any particular case. Emmet in a footnote recalls *"the answer reputed to have been given by that great teacher Father Kelly of the Society of the Sacred Mission, when asked by an earnest student at a conference, "How do we know what the Will of God really is?" − "We don't, and that's the giddy joke." (p.290)*. Brother de Kerchvel recalls a novice master saying to him *"You have got a vocation but it's not in a very healthy state."* (Butler 1999, p.141)

The respondents in this study found it difficult to explain the call to holy orders even when an interviewer spoke in terms of 'your holy orders', a kind of call to the regiment.

> *"I felt a calling to be a priest. It's difficult to describe. It has come over many years. I first thought of it when I was around 18 or 19. I believe the Gospel message has something to say today about justice and peace for the marginalised. I think it's something I think God has called me to share. The question was always celibacy and the commitment there and the whole thing about authority and the Church's teaching − the priest has to teach what the Church officially teaches."* (Newly ordained)

The idea of calling as directed towards a particular work of social reconstruction is echoed by someone no longer officially ministering:

> *"I was led by a sense of mission to build a better world founded on my Christian faith."*

Whatever the work to which the priest felt called, there was general agreement that the reason to seek ordination was not to be found in what one parish priest described as a conversion experience.

> *"We get a calling, but I didn't see the light or anything like that."* (Parish priest)

Two major sets of reasons for becoming a priest emerge from the interviews: respondents point to a network of benign cultural and family influences, or to initial resistance to the idea of priesthood.

> *"I grew up with this idea as a small boy. I became an altar server at 8. I grew up in a Catholic family in a Catholic area. The Church was the centre of our lives. Mass was part of community life. We didn't have the hang-ups people have nowadays about whether to go to mass; it was part of the culture of the time. In my parish there were always 6 or 7 boys going off to the Church."* (Non-parochial)

> *"I grew up in a very Catholic family where priests were respected. My uncle and cousin were priests."* (Parish priest)

> *"There was clericalism in the family... I was in a Catholic boarding school and being taught by priests. I think that from the age of 11 or 12 it was a fairly consistent idea."* (Bishop)

Additionally, some pointed to the example of priests in general or of particular priests:

> *"I saw priests who seemed to have something I wanted that you could not pinpoint, but something special I wanted."* (Seminarian)

> *"I came from a practising Catholic family and I had always gone to Church. I think it was the influence of certain priests, and one in particular, which led me to think about priesthood in the first place and led me to pursue it."* (Parish priest)

In these instances the idea of priesthood seems to arise almost naturally, as it were, from a distinctive way of life that is no longer pursued. Hornsby-Smith (1989) also suggests that entering the priesthood emerged as *"a natural process in their life history"*. (p.145) Fr. Foristal talks of drifting into priesthood because *"the most fulfilling possible vocation was to be a priest." "It was just... if you believe in God, if you believe in the Eucharist, if you believe in the people of God... that seemed the best thing to do"*. (Butler 1999, p.156) Other priests, however, record an experience of struggle against the idea of priesthood.

a distinctive way of life

> *"I was deeply drawn towards the priesthood. Vocation is a hard thing to describe. I thought about it a long time, but I did not*

respond until I was 21 and even then I spent over a year in discernment. For me it was not something that would go away." (Seminarian)

"It was like an itch that will not go away; it kept coming back all the time." (Non-parochial)

"It is a nudge that will not go away until eventually you have got to do something about it." (Non-parochial)

"Vocation is a hard thing to describe. There is a deep draw towards priesthood, it is not a spur of the moment thing. I thought of this a long time ago but I did not actually respond."
(Seminarian)

struggle and resistance

It is this sense of struggle and resistance that leads some to an implicit criticism of the formulation of the question: what led you to **seek** holy orders?

"In a sense I wouldn't say that I decided to be a priest. I had to go along with things because I still didn't think I would get through it (seminary training)."

"It was something inside me. Something I struggled with for a long time. I was about 14 when I first thought about it because of two little old men from a missionary society. Something connected but I didn't want to look at it… I don't think anything really attracted me to it because the priest is seen as a lonely authority figure outside the parish community, very strict and religious. The only way I could understand what God was calling me to was to try my vocation." (Seminarian)

For this student and for others it was ultimately for the Church authorities to decide on their admission to the priesthood. Fr. Radcliffe, Master of the Dominican Order states that his ordination *"was a response to a request of my brethren… you are a priest because you are asked to be so by your community."* (Butler, 1999, p.17)

Changes effected at and through ordination
Some respondents believe that at ordination they are changed at the level of being.

> *"It is an ontological change… involving a constant development of your being, conforming yourself to Christ."* (Seminarian)
>
> *"The sacraments bestow a particular seal; a spiritual demarcation as for baptism."* (Non-parochial)
>
> *"It made a mark on the soul."* (Resigned)
>
> *"There was an ontological change in my being. Just as baptism imprints on our soul and conforms us to Christ, Holy Orders deepens that conformity of likeness to Christ."* (Recently ordained)
>
> *"The Church teaches that we are different in a spiritual sense."* (Non-parochial)
>
> *"I believe that in the deepest part of our being we are changed, marked and consecrated. The ontological change brings us closer to Christ who we are called to imitate."* (Recently ordained)

an ontological change

Others prefer to see any change in terms of actual behaviour, attitude and self-concept requiring consolidation over a period of time.

change of actual behaviour

> *"It's not magical. You are still the same person. You may direct yourself in a different way. You perhaps give more time to thought about prayer and spiritual things. Like any sacrament you don't automatically change. You have to work at it."* (Parish priest)
>
> *"There is no change in my personality, my view of the world, any more than with baptism or any other sacrament… what will happen is that the grace of God will slowly work in your life if you are faithful."* (Parish priest)
>
> *"It changes me in that it gives me the authority to do certain things. It doesn't necessarily change me as an individual unless I choose to let it. In the eyes of most Catholics I have the authority to be the key person in the celebration of the sacraments and also a key person in the teaching of the Church, but I'm not too happy about that."* (Non-parochial)
>
> *"Perhaps there's a change at the beginning. You feel holy with your soutane but after a few years it doesn't matter. Priesthood is a different way of life socially."* (Parish priest)

> *"There is quite definite change. It brings stability to the person, inner strength, confidence, identity. On the religious side it gives you grace, the ability to do what others cannot, such as consecrate, absolve and so forth."* (Newly ordained)

Whether change is viewed as an immediate effect of ordination or as a longer term objective, respondents are agreed that assuming the status of priest has a number of consequences.

> *"The ordained are also part of the common priesthood. We receive a special mark. We are empowered to celebrate the sacraments unlike lay people. It's not just functional, it's ontological. Even if we no longer carried out the functions, we would still be men apart."* (Parish priest)

> *"Tradition from earliest days is that all the faithful share the priesthood of Christ, and from some of these faithful the Church chooses those to share in the ministerial priesthood. If there was no difference, there would be no priesthood."* (Parish priest)

> *"The priest is going to be central because he is the only one with the power of orders to make the sacraments become a reality. Sacraments feed the Christians. Whoever is at the heart of the sacraments is at the heart of the life of the people. Because we have the sacramental power that others want, then we are given deference or an inordinate amount of love."* (Parish priest)

power and prestige

This power and prestige can have negative consequences and lead to subtle kinds of temptation.

> *"I don't like clericalism. People can treat you in a special way when you wear a collar... when you allow yourself to be put on a pedestal, you shame other people."* (Non parochial)

> *"Ordination does not make you superior, but separate. People expect you to have virtues... they expect standards from a priest."* (Parish priest)

> *"People are always conscious of you being a priest. One has to be more circumspect in the things one does and the things one says. When holding together that (closely knit communion which is the Body of Christ) you can't always be what you*

want. Expectations from the community are that priest can't say certain things. One has to be very careful of being tempted to dominate, be in charge. One can do that in subtle ways... you are given an immense amount of power and I am amazed at the respect people have for the priesthood, for all the priests, for the role, so you mustn't get big-headed about it." (Newly ordained)

Such circumspection has consequences for those who see the objective of priesthood in terms of 'being oneself'.

Others draw attention to the consequences of another sacrament, baptism, leading to a greater equality between priests and people.

"The fundamental question would be how does baptism change you. One's character is not taken away but in response to God we have a call that enables us to reach the potential which is there for all. Holy Orders must be seen in the context of all the baptised because one who is ordained is first and foremost a Christian through baptism. Ordination is a particular sharing on the ministry of service, the priesthood of Christ for the good of the whole Church. There is a sense of all of us on a journey of faith, still searching for God. Priesthood is the way God has wanted me to respond to him. There is a change within oneself because one is responding to God, but this would also refer to someone responding to God in their particular way, for example in confirmation." (Newly ordained)

greater equality between priests and people

Finally, there are those who do see the difference conveyed through ordination in terms of job description.

"You cannot say you are holier. There's a different job to be done, as nursing is different from banking. In the past the difference would be higher/lower. The secular priesthood is a priesthood of jobs of work, ultimately to help the bishop."

(Parish priest)

Seminary life and part-life

We should note that in the present study three of the recently ordained priests, who were former Anglican priests, had not experienced seminary education. More significantly, several participants attended the seminaries of a former age. Yet their view of seminary life and of the relation between 'theory and practice' echo the opinions of more recently ordained priests.

an encouragement to immaturity

Life in a seminary is criticised in terms of an encouragement to immaturity, and its encapsulation from any life that can be counted as real.

> *"I think it was good for the time (about 30 years ago). It wouldn't suit now. Students spend more time in parishes before ordination now. I think that is good. You aren't locked away – you are aware of what is going on in the world around you, also because the seminaries are attached to universities."*
> (Parish priest)

A view that we are all on the same journey is reflected in the belief that what priests can learn from the laity is not so much an unfamiliar expertise but a firm sense of the real world.

> *"I think principally they could help the priests because the terrible danger of the clergy, principally the Catholic clergy… is living in the sociological realm of a privileged class. It is a very, very dangerous thing, it undermines one's sense of reality… if a man does not have to earn his living in a competitive world and if they're not under a threat of dismissal and so on, they can become so unreal in their attitude to the world, and I think that is the principal thing that they need to learn from lay people."* (Resigned)

Those who view their training very negatively were in formation programmes many years ago, as the two following observations indicate:

> *"It was very strict in seminary. You were allowed out once a week for a compulsory walk. The only time I went out alone in six years was to go to the dentist. I don't know anybody who would put up with a life like that."* (Parish priest)

> *"The seminary was very antiquated and was in a sorry state. Vatican II had just come in and there was a lot of unhappiness. The only way I benefited was that it taught me patience. The majority of it was a waste of time. Totally irrelevant."*

This complete dismissal is tempered by those contrasting immediate and long-term relevance and by those who view seminary education primarily in terms of a specific interior priestly spirituality.

A bishop thought that his priestly formation was *"immediately... hardly relevant at all, but long term it was very relevant... you do a lot of theology at university and you don't apply it but it's there. It becomes part of your equipment... you do learn principles and that's important."* Others seem to compress theology into the acquisition of a spirituality and of the enduring discipline of prayer:

> *"In one sense [formation] was very good. It gave you a basis of spirituality and prayer. It didn't give you a Reader's Digest approach to theology. You came out with a broad approach, not to be judgmental. It has changed massively but the fundamental idea of taking a young person for six or seven years is good."* (Parish priest)

> *"I had a good theology course, and I came out knowing more or less what I should know. They taught me to pray, they taught me the need to pray and the regularity of it, which has been a good standby for me."* (Parish priest)

> *"Where I was studying, which was abroad, we missed out on practical aspects... nevertheless it was tremendous fun; I learnt a lot, I learnt about the basic tools... how to pray and the importance of prayer... and discipline, which I think probably the modern seminary doesn't do in the same way... we had a very rigid timetable, the timetable was the same as it had been in Cardinal Wiseman's day... [the first Archbishop of Westminster] and if you do that for seven years it's a habit that dies hard... it incorporated the life of a priest and the work of a priest as inextricably bound up with a life of prayer..."*
> (Bishop)

the importance of prayer

Explorations of prayer and praying as a 'tool' that a person can use (or not) in the context of personal knowledge (Polanyi, 1958) would be rewarding, particularly in relation to the role of commitment.

Some priests believe that life for the present day seminarian has become too comfortable, but the seminary system still attracts the

the effects of alienation

criticism of an earlier time. A seminarian spoke of the initial shock experienced when first coming to his seminary. A recently ordained priest described the effects of alienation on entering a middle class world.

> *"Seminary was a middle-class institution which had nothing to do with my background or the people I am serving... we really need to change it. Long gone are the days of 120 men living a semi-monastic lifestyle. It's not healthy."* (Recently ordained)

> *"The seminary system goes back to the post-Reformation world and we live in such a different world. The cloistered and insular life is a special vocation which I don't think is mine, or your average priest or seminarian's"* (Seminarian)

> *"A lot of the system isn't conducive to a happy lifestyle – the rules, the pettiness, being told you have to be in by a certain time... I've seen men who've had their own families frustrated and feeling patronised. I think that it is a bad thing because we are offering ourselves, our lives, to be of service and you get this kind of abuse really. I'd like to see much more autonomy for the students, more responsibility."* (Recently ordained)

This indicated one possible consequence of the fact that seminarians now enter at an older age and often with prior experience in business or professional life, namely the underestimation of the abilities of mature students. As one seminarian put it:

> *"I don't think my abilities are completely utilised: men here have been teachers, run businesses, been in trade, professionals, academics – there are a lot of skills. I can think of courses I've been in I could have taught better myself."*

These and other criticisms lead some to advocate the closure of the seminary system.

closure of the seminary system

> *"You should get rid of seminaries for a start. They have outlived their useful purpose in the formation sense. [Although] you still have to give theological training. It could be co-ordinated in a central place. I think the seminarians are very*

> *cocooned, they don't experience reality, or the modern world. If you are set aside, you will find it difficult to re-engage."*
>
> (Resigned)

Possible difficulty in re-entering the post-seminary world is echoed by a seminarian who drew attention to the institutionalising effects of the system:

> *"You begin to feel institutionalised – you need more experience of other people's beliefs and conceptions of the Church. You are going to face them once ordained and you may struggle to cope."*

The importance of priests getting to know each other leads one parish priest to urge the closing down of the seminaries.

> *"I would close all seminaries down... they're expensive places to run. I would spend most of that time somewhere like this city where you could live in this house, with the priest, go to university to do some of your course, they would have to then stay at least two months every year, go to one of these seminaries, or one of these places that used to be a seminary, and meet together, talk together, pray together, get to know each other..."* (Parish priest)

The isolated location of many seminaries and the enclosed life carried on in them concretely embodied the significance of priesthood as a whole life lived wholly apart.

Theory and practice

Five aspects of the interaction between theory and practice in seminary training are illuminated in the answers of participants to a range of questions on formation: training is insufficiently practical, the specific changes required, the balance between human and priestly training, the place of 'new' topics, and formation after ordination. Training can be viewed very positively but still be judged wanting because it presents an idealised picture of the world.

> *"They prepare you in an ideal way in a seminary... little plants being nurtured and grown in a hot house, wonderful, but they send you out into a parish where they don't treat you like*

an idealised picture

that at all... The reality is you have to go and live with some parish priest who is old enough to be your grandfather... and of a different mindset altogether, and each parish has its own joys and its own problems." (Parish priest)

emphasis on academic development

Others believe that fault lies with the emphasis on academic development:

"It wasn't relevant in that it wasn't practical but academic formation." (Parish priest)

"A lot was theory, which is fine if you are going to spend your life reading books." (Resigned)

"It was not relevant to what I went into. When I came out you learn from experience. You learn more from experience than from a textbook." (Parish priest)

"I think there is too much emphasis on academic development in seminaries. I would have greater emphasis on personal development, human development..." (Bishop)

"I had to learn a lot of canon law which was changed year after year – irrelevant." (Parish priest)

The comparative emphasis on 'the practical' is taken up by those who would advocate changes in the training of priests. They would support changes predominantly in what they would describe as pastoral formation. They want to give this more time and emphasis in the training programme, alongside a reduction of the academic disciplines, in order to have, at the least, a balanced programme. Many placed a greater emphasis on practical life; to have greater experience of presbytery life and indeed the local community, to experience real lives and problems, meeting lay people, which would not only help when they were ordained priest, but who it was felt would contribute to their human development also. One participant believed the seminarians should have exposure to different organisations e.g. Amnesty International, and would like to see formation encourage more secondments and work placements.

"In priesthood you aren't going to do essays and seminars. It is important to have that knowledge, but when are we going to use some of these academic things we learn?" (Seminarian)

spiritual formation

More emphasis on spiritual formation was required by only a few participants. Pastoral studies should not 'overtake' the very important place for developing an individual spiritual life in order to face any future problems of faith.

> "The Second Vatican Council called for a year of spirituality where people would be introduced to the history of spirituality – this doesn't exist in the seminary I went to and many others. It is a terribly important thing to sustain a priest, particularly in time of difficulty so that they can grow in the priestly life."
>
> (Parish priest)

This is by no means the first reference we have had to 'spirituality' but an examination of the ways in which respondents use it reveals no clear and adequate idea of what it means.

Used on its own it seems to refer to prayer and the life and discipline of prayer which above all sustain a priest's spirit. Spirituality can, of course, be seen as emerging from the charism of figures such as St. Ignatius or St. Francis, but this sense could not be found in the replies in the present study. What can be found is a coupling and qualification of 'spirituality' which increases puzzlement; and a use of the term in practical argument concerning the role of the priest. These will be considered in turn.

When notions of the spiritual are coupled with another term it is difficult to disentangle the two. So, what is to be made of *"my faith or spiritual understanding"*; *"the theological and spiritual areas"*; the priest as spiritual and pastoral leader; *"the spiritual side of the sacraments"*; the description of a priest as *"a very spiritual man, a very good man"*? Similarly, how are we to understand spiritual when applied to values, strength, development, growth and needs?

Spirituality and 'spiritual' are also used to clarify the particular role to be played by the priest. One respondent thought that a qualified lay person should be able to overrule the parish priest (question C8) *"as long as it does not affect the spiritual side"*. Another dismissed any idea of control of his career development (question E9) with the assertion that *"spiritual development"* was all that mattered. A third, asked about formation in relationships, working collaboratively, and so on (question E3) replied that *"spiritually, you'd be tempted to say none is important."*

Most participants when asked about topic areas that should be included referred to financial training, general business training, civil law, cookery, communication and lifestyle studies. Furthermore, participants felt it important to involve more lay people in formation, including more women, for example attending lectures alongside lay people. They also believed lay professionals should be invited to lecture. The feeling among the majority of respondents was that seminarians should train with their lay peers, not apart from them. A few seminarians did not think changes were needed to formation and a very few other participants found it difficult to give an answer to the question of what changes were required: without a great deal of contemplation.

human as contrasted with priestly formation

On the important balance between human as contrasted with priestly formation the majority expressed a feeling that the human formation of a priest was not encouraged as much as priestly formation, but were aware (or at least hoped) that this is now a major issue in seminaries and that much attention is being given to developing this programme. The newly ordained priests and seminarians confirmed that human development is now a large part of formation, though some were divided on whether this was still sufficient.

> *"It [pastoral studies] is developing. There is a concern for friendship and openness. At one time seminarians would never leave the seminary – now they go to the theatre, cinema, do sports."* (Recently ordained)

> *"At one stage it seemed a very academic environment, maybe without considering human emotional development, almost as if you're a priest. I think that has improved a lot in seminaries."* (Recently ordained)

> *"Human formation is a major factor here, to develop ourselves."* (Seminarian)

> *"There is a major emphasis now on human formation. They have human development conferences each year, it's a retreat for a week with a specific theme – like sexuality, celibacy and how we express sexuality. And things like friendships, relationships, hobbies. Everything that can be used to form you to be the most*

that you can be as a person... The whole emphasis is on forming you, they say, to be firstly a person, then a Christian and a disciple." (Seminarian)

Human formation was considered extremely important, not only for dealing with lay people but also for the priest himself. This sentiment was expressed particularly strongly by the priests who have resigned their active ministry: human emotions of the priest were rarely talked about during their formation. The emphasis was on the importance of the role of the priest, rather than the priest as a human being himself.

the priest as a human being

"I wouldn't distinguish between a human and a priest — a priest is a human being and a part of the laity before he is a priest... The priest although celibate, he is a sexual human being — he's a human who supports a football team as well. The most important thing you bring to the priesthood is your inadequacies. (Parish priest)

"The Church has neglected the human in favour of the priestly and the supernatural. This is one of the chief problems of the Church especially with sex. The whole picture is clouded by anti-humanism and 'angelism' — the attempt to pretend we aren't human, that we don't have human functions, that we're pure spirits, it is putting priests on a pedestal as if free from human faults. I think it is precisely the neglect of the human that is bedevilling the Church and is behind a lot of the troubles, especially child abuse and intellectual ignorance."
(Resigned)

"There is not a great deal on coping with awkward situations, emotional problems that may arise... it's a very male-orientated situation. I don't think there was enough preparation to examine thoroughly how you would cope with celibacy."
(Resigned)

"In many priests, qualities such as loyalty and fruitfulness are not as pronounced as they might be. There is too much insistence in seminary on aspects of spirituality — prayers, the Office — more than anything else. I know priests who have had nervous breakdowns." (Resigned)

One wonders about the preparation of future priests for situations of loss and mourning when the departure of a fellow student was left starkly unexplained.

> *"I think that in my day human formation, emotion, loneliness, success, human affections for other people were not talked about. People left the seminary, you went to meditation, came back and you found the man's room was completely stripped and empty, that was the end of it, he just went out of your existence. Clearly the order was, if you ever expressed any doubts about your vocation the first order was you don't share these doubts with anyone, we will remove you, and they went, like that."* (Resigned)

New areas in formation

The place of 'new' areas to be covered in formation was investigated by showing participants a card (Card C) with a number of subject areas and asking for a view on the relative merits of each. The subject areas were: relationships, child protection, communication skills, groupwork/teamwork skills, working collaboratively, chaplaincy training, finance and administration.

Almost all participants agreed that these areas should to some extent be included in the training programme, and that several were related to each other. Indeed many spoke of the subjects together as a collective programme. Few participants considered that any areas were irrelevant. Some were felt to be currently fashionable, but this did not lessen their importance as crucial and important subjects for the future of the Church. Participants wanted priests to be given a fuller and more realistic vision and experience of the problems they might experience. Many participants acknowledged that these subjects were currently taught in seminary already.

Each subject area will now be discussed.

Relationships

Relationships were considered to be of profound importance to the job of the priest, and essentially a basic skill requirement.

> *"I was very immature with relationships. At 27 I hadn't matured, I didn't deal with relationships, I was handling relationships like a 16 year old.* (Resigned)

> *"Every priest I have worked with has been immature when it comes to relationships. Basically because Catholic families find it a great status to have a priest. Many priests I know find it difficult to relate to other people, feel set apart"* (Resigned)

Those set in a pedestal or who see themselves as essentially men apart may see no need for relationships.

Participants suggested that part of the priest's job now is primarily to have different types of relationships with many different types of people; male and female, young and old. Learning to relate to them, learning to interpret behaviour, and dealing with problems which may arise were all very important.

learning to relate

> *"Priesthood is ultimately a relationship with people. It would give you a good grounding to know how people react, to interpret behaviour and draw attention to things you might otherwise not see."* (Seminarian)

> *"Certainly that is necessary for a priest in a parish to be able to relate and communicate."* (Parish priest)

> *"I think [relationships] is important… In the seminary… there's no sense whatsoever in which you are helping other people or they are helping you… as far as relationships were concerned the whole thing was on ice, they were looking ahead to say there must be no suggestion of a relationship with a woman, they are always scared to death of homosexuality in an all male community, and anything like friendship or intimacy was absolutely discouraged…"* (Resigned)

However, a few respondents questioned how building relationships could be taught successfully: is it an intrinsic skill one is born with?

> *"Can you teach people to make relationships? You can encourage people to make relationships, you can pick them up when they go wrong, you can affirm them, but actually teaching them?"* (Bishop)

"Relationships is the most difficult because I think you're born with that it's like having a course on how to fall in love… some people are very good at having relationships, some people are not. Some priests are lonesome men, because that's their nature, that's the way they are, and I don't think any amount of talking would necessarily change them." (Parish priest)

We should distinguish, of course, between solitariness and loneliness.

Child protection

Turning to child protection, many commented that this area of training was now, unfortunately, a very necessary part of the priest's training: the priest must be conscious of all the legislation and official procedures regarding child protection.

"That's necessary nowadays, just as it is for teachers. It should be done in seminary and independently in the diocese so they are told exactly what the procedures are and what their role is. It's absolutely essential." (Parish priest)

The priest is regarded as a figure of authority in the community, alongside other professionals such as teachers and doctors, and therefore must be versed in procedure, he has to be able to act in a professional manner and always be accountable for his actions, if only to provide protection for himself.

"It is crucial for anyone working around children. People have to be very careful as much for their safety as the child." (Resigned)

"We must be professional and accountable in our relationships with people now because everybody else is e.g. teachers/doctors."
(Recently ordained)

The newly ordained and seminarians mentioned they do currently receive training on this subject.

Several participants pointed out that they did not wish priests to become wary of approaching children, and would still hope to maintain a caring attitude.

"To be aware of [child protection] but not to get people so

cramped that they never put their hand on a child... if a little girl comes running up to me, I'm not going to push her away but give her a hug." (Bishop)

Communication

Communication skills were thought to be useful not only when talking to different people, across different generations, but also in church, on other occasions when addressing the public, or even when talking to the media. To be able to communicate with others on a professional or more casual basis, to be able to adapt to different situations was considered very important for priests. *"You can't talk religion all the time"*, as one respondent put it. Ultimately, in a leadership role, the priest must have the ability to communicate the message of the Gospel.

> *"It has to be included – dealing with people – young lads, teenagers – all generations."* (Resigned)

> *"People expect good communication. We should make use of professional teachers. We should take advantage of any training offered, for example in television or radio."* (Parish priest)

> *"You need to be able to shift gear and put on different hats in social communication."* (Recently ordained)

Groupwork

Again the skills of groupwork, teamwork and working collaboratively were felt to improve the relationships priests have with other members of the Church, the laity, committees or the wider community. Participants often mentioned that the priest was not always the leader of working groups, but had to learn skills such as delegation, group management and decision making. Others were also looking to a future of merged parishes and working closely with members of different parishes.

> *"It is essential to work with others in the parish. You're not the boss, you share the mission."* (Seminarian)

> *"In the future this will be important. When the number of priests go down and they merge parishes."* (Parish priest)

> *"It is essential with people in the community and community groups – it's people working for the good of everyone."* (Resigned)

Chaplaincy work

Working outside the parish environment as chaplains, within hospitals, prisons or schools, was seen to involve a different discipline and different pressures from working in a parish. Priests had little idea exactly what to expect in these (often difficult) situations, so experience of these environments through pastoral work was considered essential.

> *"It depends on what you are doing. It can be extremely difficult to be a chaplain."* (Resigned)

> *"The danger has been (the attitude) that if you are a priest you can do everything."* (Resigned)

> *"I'm chaplain of a local high school. I didn't receive any training – I was thrown in at the deep end… It's a specific thing to become a chaplain – I think that sort of training should be given once you're appointed."* (Recently ordained)

Finance and administration

Many priests mentioned they had little knowledge of book keeping, and often found it hard to do the parish accounts: some training certainly would be welcome in this area. Others felt this was an area for lay expertise and was not a crucial area of priestly formation.

> *"Well it is a specialism, if in a short space of time you can give them an idea, then so much the better… I think the priest should have some sort of money sense."* (Bishop)

> *"It's not really an essential feature of formation. You can get lay people involved if they have those skills. It doesn't have to be the domain of priests."* (Seminarian)

> *"We have sufficient laity qualified to take over the responsibility of finance."* (Parish priest)

Increasingly priests have to deal with more and more administration. As for financial training, it was thought to be an area where basic training would be useful, but which should be left largely to lay people in the parish.

> *"Admin should be an element of formation, but people in parishes can do that."* (Seminarian)

The majority of participants felt strongly that all the subjects discussed were crucial for the future of the church. While some considered these 'fashionable subjects' they did not feel this decreased their usefulness.

> "Crucial. I don't think we can survive without formation in those things." (Parish priest)

> "There are fads about these things but there are certain basics in all these areas that need to be dealt with." (Parish priest)

> "They are all vitally important, but it's more important to get down to the fundamentals of the priestly ministry, which is the proclamation of the Gospels and being secure in faith."
> (Recently ordained)

Need for continuing formation

Many older participants, and those who have resigned their active ministry, mentioned they had had little or no formal continuing training, and this was considered a serious gap. Although some reported that their everyday life and contact with different people, and difficult situations, was a constant educational experience, there was a call for a more formally structured approach to formation throughout a priest's life. A formal guaranteed process was felt to be essential and appropriate as with many other jobs, in order to keep up with contemporary issues and new situations.

a more formally structured approach

> "It's important for recently ordained priests to meet regularly (every couple of months) to discuss issues. Nobody's talking to each other. We get ordained and just have to get on with it for the rest of our lives until we drop…! You are caring for everyone else, but you're not caring for yourself in some ways. I think priests burn out, they just get fed up with it. There is no one to talk to about these things. Also meeting older priests and finding out how they cope." (Recently ordained)

no one to talk to

> "I think it's important to keep people up to date. We don't have time to read the latest things and keep up to date. We need to be aware of big issues being discussed, and be more informed about those." (Parish priest)

> "When I left to work in insurance, we had training every month. Once a year we would sit an exam in our particular areas. If we failed we would be suspended from working. I know priests who have left seminary and not read another book since." (Resigned)

> "I asked for help and I felt very isolated and I could understand why people do have relationships. Ongoing training was non-existent. I was a priest for going on three years and I didn't go on one training course in those three years." (Resigned)

Certainly continuing formation was an important expectation for the seminarians in this research.

> "I think formation should be a constant part of your ministry – new situations and issues will always arise."

> "I think it is something which is quite important. Especially to keep in touch after ordination, to ensure you are giving the best possible service."

> "After seminary? I expect I will continue formation, because I carry on living and the world changes."

Many other participants reported training days and annual retreats were offered in their dioceses.

> "It's up to you to see what you can do to enhance your formation. We are informed of workshops and courses. I do as many as I can because it gives me an insight into what is going on." (Recently ordained)

> "In this diocese there is an on-going programme of formation and there is a diocesan priestly retreat once a year which is about a week in length. There are two or three days set aside. We have a priest who has a specific ministry to priests which is spiritual as well as pastoral, and we are encouraged by the diocese to make a personal retreat." (Recently ordained)

Some priests reported that time constraints, and what they considered to be 'irrelevant' courses prevented them from attending continuing formation. Those who did attend courses appreciated the effort involved, but reported there was room for improvement. They suggested more study days, a variety of courses to choose from, and a higher standard of teaching.

> "The diocese has a very good programme on further training e.g. days on aspects of church teaching or pastoral ministry. The problem is accessibility. In a busy parish the attitude is 'we can't have Mass because the priest is away'. I feel guilty leaving the parish priest to do two Masses. I'd love to do a lot of study, counselling skills, or applied theology. It's finding time."
> (Recently ordained)

> "We do have ongoing formation in this diocese but unfortunately I find the issues not particularly relevant. I go to some of them. I applaud them for the effort, I am glad something is being done but I am not satisfied." (Recently ordained)

> "Sadly there are no courses for school chaplains – hospitals and prisons. I toyed with going on a two day course but I thought it wouldn't be relevant… the real use is not so much the things you learn but the mixing with people who serve the church like yourself." (Recently ordained)

> "I feel that they don't address the fundamental and the crucial issues. I'm not opposed to it at all in principle. I think it is an extremely good idea but in practice I haven't found it particularly helpful." (Parish priest)

> "We get in-service training days – it is fairly satisfactory. It could be better, we could have more study days." (Parish priest)

> "We have had very poor in-service training. We have to go on retreat every other year. That is good, but they get all these clever fellow from the religious orders." (Parish priest)

However, the bishops in this study were concerned that when training days are offered, priests fail to turn up. They recognised this may be part of a larger cultural problem.

priests fail to turn up

> "It's very unsatisfactory… it's the whole culture thing that has got to be changed. I think priests are very tired at the end of six years' training. It's a very long training. And we have not got in place a regular expectation of highly skilled good quality training from then onwards." (Bishop)

> *"We need to get people to do it. Motivate people… they leave the seminary and that's it… there's the strictly academic areas… a lot of these things are things people say that they need, but it's one thing to say that they need it, and it's another thing when you put it on for them to go to… so that's the climate and sort of culture where we are interested enough in our ministry that we need it… we haven't developed a structure to make it compulsory."* (Bishop)

One participant felt the onus to participate should be on the priests themselves and that the reason for non-attendance was a lack of interest:

> *"If you go to your doctor or dentist or lawyer, you hope they are up to date with the latest techniques, and isn't just carrying on with what they learnt in 1950… It's only recently that the clergy have thought it desirable to take refresher courses. Very few of them really take it seriously."* (Resigned)

the inclusion of lay people

The inclusion of lay people in the continuing formation of a priest was felt to be vital. Certainly lay professionals were seen to be the greatest source for teaching on various subjects such as child protection, counselling skills, and finance. Many acknowledged that lay people would know much more than they would themselves, both in social and professional subjects, and these specialities should be utilised for the good of the Church. Others thought that the lay people with whom they came into daily contact would provide a continuing formation through social contact, communication and encountering different situations, outside a formal course or lecture.

> *"As far as the present Church is concerned, with a celibate clergy, endlessly trying to drum into their heads what is involved in marriage and the up-bringing of children and the responsibilities and so on… in an ideal church there are bound to be areas about which lay people have much more experience than the clergy."* (Resigned)

> *"In so far as their professional skills and competency is relevant to aspects touching priestly life, that is to say for example these issues of dealing with children, with finance, yes."* (Parish priest)

> *"They have much more to say than anyone else in certain areas. Priests want to know how to manage married people, or catechesis and teaching religion to children, or general evangelisation. I've been on events run by lay people and they have been very good — they have a very fresh approach and a depth of expertise..."* (Parish priest)

The majority of participants thought it would be a positive idea if lay people and priests could attend courses together. Interaction and feedback with lay people would create a healthy environment in which to learn. Indeed, participants mentioned this practice was already common in seminaries and dioceses and worked very successfully.

> *"It's a good idea. We can learn from each other. We are all on a journey together."* (Recently ordained)

> *"We are all human beings striving for the same thing. If we are working together we should be able to do those courses together."* (Parish priest)

> *"I would fully agree. I have attended courses with the laity on marriage, marriage preparation with doctors and nurses."* (Parish priest)

Expectations of priesthood and whether they were met

Both those in the active ministry and seminarians refer to their expectations, past and present in highly abstract non-specific terms, as if attaining priesthood was an end in itself, one certainty in a troubled and uncertain world.

> *"I expect to love and serve God and give that love and service to other people in the Church. I hope if I ever get ordained it will be a life of joy and happiness, but I am realistic to know that won't always be the case. I expect it will be hard because we are living in a society where it might seem God has no place and because a priest has no place in that society. I expect a time of learning, of looking to new ground where we can bring God to people. It will be a time of constant re-learning and challenge, of facing a new horizon and we don't really know where we are going. You're scared of where you are going."* (Seminarian)

> "I expected a good, wholesome life style and to do things that were special. There was also an element of being respected."
> (Newly ordained)

> "I did not have any clear expectations. This was probably just as well because nothing works out as you expect. I'm not an agoniser I just get on with what I have to do." (Parish priest)

> "It was into the unknown, you weren't planning that you'd be this priest or that priest. You were just trying to pursue a sense of vocation and direct life towards it." (Parish priest)

> "I had no explicit expectations... I felt I was doing the right thing." (Resigned)

One respondent recalled that his seminary rector discouraged them from entertaining any expectations since they would not be met.

obedience to the bishop

For others the expectations were much more specific, either in terms of obedience to the bishop or carrying out the usual functions of a priest.

> "I expected that it would be a life dedicated to the service of the Church and people. My expectation is to do whatever the bishop asks." (Recently ordained)

> "You are obedient to the bishop, you are celibate. Obviously the way you lead your life and the way you behave changes."
> (Recently ordained)

> "My expectations were that you say Mass, visit people, that there is a lot of day-to-day administration. That is pretty much the way it is." (Non-parochial)

> "I expected to be a priest: to say Mass, to celebrate the sacraments and to encourage people to be holy." (Bishop)

personal costs as well as benefits

Others reported that they had entered the priesthood or were studying for it with an expectation of personal costs as well as benefits.

> "I expected to make sacrifices. It was a vocation not a profession." (Non-parochial)

"There is an element of sacrifice. For example, on New Year's Eve I was called out twice in the night because someone was dying. There are not many occupations where you would be on duty like that." (Recently ordained)

"It is emotionally demanding, you are faced with contrasting situations in short spaces of time... you have to give of yourself a lot and have energy." (Seminarian)

On the whole the majority of serving priests (i.e. bishops, newly ordained, parochial and non-parochial priests) tended to report that their general expectations had been met, and in some cases exceeded.

expectations exceeded

"My expectation was to carry out the ministry along the lines the Lord has indicated... that has been met to a considerable extent." (Parish priest)

"I would say my expectations have been met. I have found my priesthood very fulfilling." (Parish priest)

"I live out that idea of service. The fruits of the work are palpable. My expectations have not only been achieved but exceeded." (Recently ordained)

"I was very much expecting what I got. I know what it entailed. It is a big commitment to be a Catholic priest. You have to be celibate and often you are living on your own. I'm quite happy." (Recently ordained)

"My expectations have been more than met. It has got more exciting as the years have gone on." (Non-parochial)

"I am not disappointed. If you put a lot into it, you get a lot back." (Non-parochial)

"I have been a priest for nearly 40 years and I'm still happy in my vocation." (Parish priest)

Any disappointments arise from three sources. First, a distinction between satisfaction at a personal level compared to a Church level. Second, the experience of those no longer in official ministry, third a corrective view of the idealistic nature of early expectations.

satisfaction at a Church level

> "My expectations have been met in that I can help people. They have not in that the Church has not moved on as I would have liked it to have done. In the 1960's we thought the Church was going to have a revolution. It did change enormously, but there was a tendency to put the brakes on."
>
> (Non-parochial)

> "In those days we were part of a Church which... wanted to grow and expand. The whole life was centred around the parish and the priest had a fundamental role within that... lots of changes have taken place and not really lived up to the expectations that we were going to continue the experience of the '50's and '60's." (Parish priest, ordained 1965)

> "Not everybody is interested in what you have to say. Priestly work is often routine, visiting the sick, baptism, daily mass. All quite repetitive. When I was younger I was looking to a revival of the Church, but now there is a continuing falling away. You wonder why and what part you played in it." (Parish priest)

It is to be expected that disappointment is most sharply expressed by those no longer exercising official priestly ministry.

> "I expected to gain a lot of strength and encouragement from the other priests... I thought they would back each other up and be ringing me up to see how I was doing. That expectation was not met at all." (Resigned)

> "I became disillusioned. As time went on it became apparent that the structures through which we worked, like the parish, diocese or schools, were all designed to be a holding operation, whereas the situation needed a missionary organisation."
>
> (Resigned)

> "I expected to serve and work with all kinds of people... my expectations changed... I knew the kinds of lines we ought to be pursuing in education and I hit a stone wall. I was told 'no' by people not as well educated or as well trained as me. I could not live in a regime where I was simply told what to do without any discussion." (Resigned)

> "I was disappointed that the Catholic Church has not adopted

Vatican II more wholeheartedly, and has gone back to the authoritarian mood of the 19th century." (Resigned)

The priesthood, as we have seen, is likely to attract idealistic aspirations, and some priests report not so much disappointment as a readjustment once the priestly life has been established.

> "I felt the priesthood would change me, that when I was ordained I would be made good enough to be what I imagined a priest should be... that was not realistic. After about five years, I had to re-evaluate my role as a priest. I found some of the clergy very supportive in that." (Non-parochial)

> "I suppose I thought I would do terrific work and bring a lot of people to a knowledge of God... I do not think those expectations have been fulfilled. Not everybody is interested in what you have got to say. (Parish priest)

> "Initially I had an idealistic idea of what it would be like. It turned out not to be, but I am not disappointed." (Parish priest)

"I had to re-evaluate my role as a priest."

Some seminarians mentioned how possible future developments in the Church might affect the meeting of expectations. A decline in the number of priests would necessitate the merging of parishes, which in turn might mean priests in the future are busier, more reliant on lay collaboration, and less likely to mix with other priests. Additionally, the integration of the Church into modern society was considered a challenge which might involve change for priests in terms of workload and priestly collegiality.

> "My reactions are mixed, given the decline in numbers. The job could change drastically over the years. Parish merging means demands are a lot higher, the role of the priest has become a lot busier."

> "If I became a priest, I would be in the thick of things with the laity. I might not see another priest for days."

> "Shifting perceptions of priests and the Church are not going to make my life easy. The Church is facing new territory it did not expect to face. It is going to be a time of challenge and re-learning how to approach society and integrate ourselves in it."

Conclusion

The term 'vocation' is ascribed only to certain kinds of occupation. These tend to be occupations with a high altruistic content and comparatively low pay, such as nursing and social work. In the case of the priests we have been studying 'vocation' is invoked as a justification for undertaking "something special", and for claiming a special closeness with Christ. Such a vocation entails meeting particular demands.

> *"People expect you to have virtues because in some way you are a leader. They expect standards from a priest."*
>
> (Parish priest)

It is a call to a whole way of life, even though the specific 'spirituality' of the parish priest remains largely undeveloped. Respondents seem to reject a notion of the call coming out of nowhere, so to speak, and of 'call' as a sudden, overwhelming demand. Instead, they seek to explain it as the result of cultural influences, and as subject to development over time. We see more dramatic conceptions in those priests who talk in terms of the ontological change brought in them at ordination. This contrasts with those who see any changes mediated through gradual developments in self-concept and through social interaction.

In view of the universal interest in the formulation of priestly charters, the perceptions and recommendations of those who have been through the seminary process and those at present in training are of particular interest. The similarity of views expressed by older and younger clergy casts doubt on the effects of recent changes, and the extent to which those responsible for the training of priests recognise the depth of societal changes and changes in the Church itself. The notion of a priest as pre-formed to a timeless Christ may not be helpful in reviewing the education or training of priests at any particular time. The idea of formation does suggest forming to a pre-conceived pattern rather than any idea of education responsive to notions of current practice and understanding. The apparent acceptance of the significance of human development as contrasted with priestly development indicates that more work needs to be done on the relationship between the two, and on priesthood as a particular way of 'being oneself'.

Chapter Four

GOVERNANCE: HOLY ORDERS AND HOLY ORDERING

THE TERMS USED to describe the interest of the Queen's Working Party – authority and governance in the Roman Catholic Church – are complex, if not contested, in the case of 'authority' and insecurely anchored in the case of 'governance'. This chapter is concerned with the latter. It discusses governance as viewed in Canon Law and as interpreted more broadly as equivalent to administration. Degrees of satisfaction and dissatisfaction with contemporary governance are then identified at different levels in the Church.

The Canon Law response

Most respondents treated 'governance' without reference to Canon Law. For them 'governance' was the equivalent of administration or management, and this rough definition enabled many, as we shall see, to argue that lay people were already fully or significantly involved in the governance of the Church. Some respondents however, did have a working knowledge of Canon Law (for example, theologians, bishops, lecturers and one canon lawyer) and they answered questions about governance in the light of Canon 129:

1. Those who are in sacred orders are, in accordance with the provisions of law, capable for the power of governance, which belongs to the church by divine institution. This power is also called the power of jurisdiction.
2. Lay members of Christ's faithful can co-operate in the exercise of this same power in accordance with the law.

Restricting the role of the laity in governance or jurisdiction to an undefined co-operation that is in accordance with the law raises the need for clarification at different levels.

> "The difficulty comes, and this is a question I don't think the theologians have answered yet, is that Canon Law says where

restricting the role of the laity

it is appropriate lay people may share in governance. But they haven't said how. And because it's so tied up with theology, because that principle of governance stems from what we believe the priest to be [representing the person of Christ] which takes us right back to the gospel, until the theologians have worked this out we can't get much further. Because the church is a magisterial church, we need the support of the magisterium to make a major step forward, and I think it's going to be a major step… I think what we've got to do is to think very seriously about the way lay people can share in the governance, and I don't think we've tackled that properly yet. And there are lots of people around who are very able to take on roles which are viewed as roles of governance… I think what we're working towards I hope is a two-tier level of government… I don't necessarily see it as two-tier but as two distinct functions. This doesn't necessarily mean that one is above the other, but they are simply different. And I think that what we've got quite well-defined is what the priestly role of governance is, but we still have a long way to go before we see what the lay role of governance is."

This response from a non-parochial priest who had training in canon law argues for further work in theology or, more precisely, ecclesiology. The denial of superiority of one tier of government over another characterises recognition of the differentiation of clergy from laity. Acknowledging as 'simply different' the demarcation in terms of function will depend on our ability to avoid a situation in which some functions are defined as more significant or more sacred than others.

problems of consistency

Canon Law also seems to present problems of consistency or logic, though these too may be perceived broadly as 'theological'.

"It would seem from one way that only those who are ordained can exercise jurisdiction. Yet on the other hand Canon Law says that a bishop can appoint a lay person to administer a parish, which is definitely exercising some kind of jurisdiction. Some people would argue that unless you are ordained you can't exercise jurisdiction. Canon Law itself would seem to say they can. So I'd say that theologically there seems to be a dispute going on here. The jury's still out on this one." (Bishop)

Finally, some argued that church life had, in some parishes at any rate, already overtaken the provisions of canon law:

> "People are only by degree getting used to taking real responsibility, but in the good parishes... the priest does nothing except sign a few cheques because it's all done for him. Canon Law is a bit behind what is actually happening." (Bishop)

Governance more broadly viewed

Most of the respondents appear to believe that governance does not belong exclusively to the priest. Not only can the laity participate but they already do so in a taken-for-granted sense.

> "In terms of governance there is a lot of lay participation in the church. Bishops have a lot of lay people advising them on finance, education, pastoral and ecumenical areas, and so on."
> (Recently ordained)

> "The laity fit in at a management, administrative, consultative, advisory level with all the experience they have. They should be involved all the way up. The Pope has consultative councils, the majority of whose members are laity. When decisions are taken, they have taken on board the advice of experts."
> (Recently ordained)

> "There is a role for lay people to play in church government. There are many lay theologians, both male and female. Lay experts must advise the bishops on medical, ethical and scientific problems before they make decisions..." (Parish priest)

> "Lay people assist in the governance of the church, yes... One of the powers traditionally which has been identified is governing, but it is not the exclusive prerogative of the priesthood." (Parish priest)

> "The Church cannot be a democracy in one sense. You can't have a vote that murder is ok. The bishops and the Pope have the authority to guide the Church. But they should use lay people in making decisions, for example, over women priests, because at the end of the day the job of the priest is to serve the Church, not the other way round." (Newly ordained)

governance does not belong exclusively to the priest

lay involvement as expert

In reviewing responses we should note the emphasis on lay involvement as justified as expert as well as the optimistic gloss on the weight this expert advice can be expected to carry. Advice accordingly is valued but opinion seems divided on how to characterise lay involvement. It can consist in a number of specific roles, liturgical and managerial to name two, or it can be viewed more broadly in terms of what is described as *"a collaborative role"*. Collaboration-talk is now common in the Catholic Church but it poses problems concerning the initiation of a collaborative response from the laity and the skills required to recognise the appropriate talents. It also reveals two different modes of listening to what lay people say. The first revolves around the politician's fashionable response, I hear what you are saying, contrasted with I understand what you are trying to communicate. The second mode of listening harks back to the rule of St. Benedict which advocates consultation and listening by the abbot on the grounds that the best course of action could be revealed to the youngest of the community.

> *"Governance in the sense of supervision and guiding development is properly in the hands of the bishop because that is an apostolic authority. But any good governor should employ the gifts of others... bishops should delegate not concentrate all power in their hands – but the final word must be with the one supreme ecclesiastical authority in the diocese."* (Parish priest)

an emphasis on delegation

An emphasis on delegation as the source of legitimacy for lay involvement places a considerable responsibility on those who choose and facilitate others to exercise delegated powers.

"Lay people can share very much [in governance]... The main teaching of Vatican II was that it's the priests and the bishops who look for the talents of their own community. They need to recognise the gifts of others and help them to use them..." Gift-spotting is not easy, however.

> *"Lay people fulfil these roles as adequately as a parish priest – that is management talents or professional skills or leadership qualities."* (Seminarian)

> *"Governance is something that lay people do do... In the parish, lay people are encouraged to take on specific roles, liturgical roles, and also to take on pastoral roles and also*

> *managerial roles. Indeed in canon law we are required to have a finance committee to look after the money that comes in. Most parishes have a parish pastoral council as well which is made up of lay people."* (Recently ordained)

Lay involvement also poses what are seen to be potential dangers which it is the responsibility of the priest to guard against.

> *"With a lot of things you delegate. The priest does not have to do everything but it is important that whatever a parish community does, does not come into conflict with what others are doing. You cannot go off on your own and the priest is there as a guide rather than the boss."* (Non-parochial)

> *"A lay Pope would be worse than an ordained Pope, because lay people treat the Church as if it is was a lay organisation, and the Church is run on totally different lines... Lay people can do most of the things we do as regards administration, but the Church does not like things run on committee lines: it wants someone to be responsible. In the past making a layman responsible has not proved successful because they are not totally committed. When you put people in charge of finance they become very mercenary... I would not want to pressurise people into giving what they could not afford. I am cautious about pressurising people to come to meetings unless they were retired."* (Non-parochial)

Satisfaction and dissatisfaction with governance in the contemporary Church

We sought not to treat *"governance"* as a unitary topic of satisfaction and the contrary, but to distinguish between different levels of governance – that of the Vatican, the local ordinary and the parish priest. It is an interesting reflection of the lay advisory role some believe is played at the diocesan and papal level that this role escaped both positive and negative evaluation. It is only at parish level that lay involvement is treated as part of governance, and even there evaluation revolves primarily around the role of the priest.

Satisfaction
Satisfaction with governance was the predominant response, even though some levels of satisfaction do not appear deeply grounded.

the predominant response

> "The Church jogs along alright. We are learning to delegate: we have deacons in the Church. We are trying to educate the Curia to be more liberal in delegating, not being so dogmatic."
> (Non-parochial)

> "I'm quite happy. To me the Church is very simple: the people of God. You don't need a lot of laws of administration, if you stick to the truth. Governance does not affect us very much. We get guidelines on the liturgy but are not tied down in a straight jacket: truth is freedom." (Parish priest)

Respondents in all categories were satisfied with governance in the contemporary Church, with the exception of those who had resigned their active ministry. It was notable overall, however, that the seminarians and the newly ordained priests were more frequently supportive of current methods but there were also parochial and non-parochial priests who expressed support for the current papacy and shared a positive view of current methods of governance. The main distinction between those generally satisfied with contemporary governance and those who were dissatisfied was that the former believed in governmental powers handed on by God through an unbroken chain.

Typically those who expressed support for the current holder of the papal office and loyalty to Rome saw the Pope as St. Peter's successor, the head of the Church and the servant of the Church, whose role bears within it both the responsibility and the grace of governance:

> "Personally I'm quite happy with the church's government... At the top I'm quite happy with the Pope at the head of the church, and all authority stems from there. The See is the successor of St. Peter... St. Peter was placed as the head of the church by Christ himself and there is that unbroken link right down the centuries. The authority stems from the papacy... The hierarchy and the Pope are ultimately responsible for teaching."
> (Recently ordained)

> "As Catholics we believe that Our Lord gave St. Peter a specific task. 'You are Peter and on this rock I will found my church' and he is the first head of the Church and from him

has been an unbroken succession of chief pastors, Popes, of apostles, bishops and of presbyters." (Recently ordained)

Others pointed out that unity was a necessary requirement, for a church centred on Christ, and this unity could only be attained and pursued through a single central authority.

unity a necessary requirement

> "There has to be a central authority because it's a church and not a collection of individuals – it's the body of Christ, a corporate unity, and within that is the supreme governance of Christ. There is apostolic authority with divine authority behind it, and its specific purpose is to govern and direct teaching and the Church... The Catholic Church is not a congregational structure – it's not a question of how many are in favour of this or that. Consequently there has to be some central direction but exercised in a spirit of service not domination." (Parish priest)

Other respondents took a similar position on the theological importance of unity of faith within the Church:

> "One thing I like about Catholicism is the centralisation of the Papacy. It holds us all together. Rome is the centre of the faith and I wouldn't want that to change." (Seminarian)

> "Some people see Cardinal Ratzinger as a challenge but I don't. I'm glad he's saying the things he's saying. If people are allowed to undermine Roman statements and guidance, things will begin to fall apart at the centre." (Recently ordained)

> "People are not listening to what the Holy Father is saying. He says a lot of good things. He has certainly stood up for what the Church teaches. You can't deny two thousand years of tradition and wisdom. And I believe in things like the magisterium, and decisions in which the Holy Spirit is involved. If we water down the teaching, people will see disunity and disharmony, and quickly leave. There is a huge element of pride in not listening. If we aren't listening, why do we stay?" (Seminarian)

That the Holy Spirit is the source of the inspired teaching of the Pope in the Church's *magisterium* was a further point which respondents made in order to explain their approval of papal governance:

> "There is always a tension between the centre and the outside, and this can be healthy, as in the family. In South America many of the priests and local communities had become involved in a political way in response to oppression. The present Pope hauled them back. Priests should not be involved in politics in this way. This is how one sees the Holy Spirit guiding the Church" (Recently ordained)

> "The Catholic Church speaks with the authority of the Holy Spirit – it isn't a debating society. I'm reasonably satisfied, recognising that the Holy Spirit is working through human material." (Non-parochial)

Very few respondents mention that lay members of the Church could be inspired.

a spirit of service

Another key point for respondents was the way in which governance was exercised. A number emphasised that governance should be exercised (and understood) within a spirit of service which is Christ-centred:

> "It's always going back to the example of Christ – the Master, but the Apostles' servant. That aspect of service is important."
> (Non-parochial)

It is obviously considered important, but it is never operationalised, particularly in western society where the notions of servant are now scarcely intelligible.

Strong and warm support for the person of John Paul II was also frequently expressed by those satisfied with governance in the contemporary church.

> "We've never had a more vigorous Pope who is not afraid to stand up and say things the world doesn't necessarily want to hear." (Recently ordained)

> "In my opinion this pontificate has revitalised the papacy to a great extent and there have been some incredible achievements."
> (Parish priest)

> *"I'm fairly happy with the universal governance of the church. The Pope is an inspirational person."* (Parish priest)

> *"I think the Pope is doing great. He is a world figure…"*
> (Non-parochial)

> *"At Vatican level I am amazed at the prodigious output of various departments of the Holy See. I think if we read them and tried to put them into practice we would carry out great work… I'm very satisfied. Pope John Paul has been an excellent governor of the Church."* (Recently ordained)

Satisfaction at the diocesan level is less clearly articulated. The personality of the local bishop can be appreciated and the range of his responsibilities acknowledged.

> *"Personally, I'm quite happy with the governance in the contemporary Church… In the diocese there could be more consultation with people with qualifications and understanding of finance. You can't expect a bishop to know everything about investments and buildings. He has to concern himself more with the spiritual side and to be a true shepherd of the flock"* (Parish priest)

Opinion can, of course, be divided.

> *"At diocesan level some say the diocese is working brilliantly. Others wish for the return of their former bishop. Some dioceses are strictly run by the bishop. The bishop has to be strict but also flexible in relation to the community of the diocese. Keeping priests happy is more difficult than anything. When I speak of strictness I mean in the sense of teaching."* (Seminarian)

Alternatively, different aspects of governance receive different evaluations:

> *"My relationship with the bishop is wonderful – Anglicans much more conscious of the lord bishop… I have a sense of bishops as one of us. In this way they get more respect and co-operation. One is not just obeying but co-operating. On the administrative level governance is very poor indeed. The Church is reactive not proactive. There is no clear thinking and

satisfaction at the diocesan level

planning even at diocesan level... The Cardinal (the late Basil Hume) is a vision man, but totally impractical." (Recently ordained)

"The local bishop is alright but sometimes retreats from working with priests to a kind of single mindeness." (Parish priest)

At the level of the parish satisfaction seems to derive from a simple application of a vocabulary of collaboration.

"At the parish level we are trying to implement collaborative ministry, in the areas of finance and instruction. People must realise that the parish belongs to them and the priest is only coming and going." (Non-parochial)

Dissatisfactions

In relation to the different levels of church governance dissatisfactions take distinct forms. At the level of the Papacy there is criticism of a style of government which drowns the authentic voice of the local bishops. By contrast bishops are criticised for showing weak leadership and insufficient support for the central authorities in Rome. At the parish level concern is expressed concerning the power of parish priests.

autocratic style

The strongest criticisms of current central government came from those no longer in active ministry, but a few current parochial and non-parochial priests were also concerned over the autocratic style they believe has been increasingly adopted in recent years. It is helpful to attempt to identify distinct strands of criticism: models of government adopted, consequences of renewed centralisation, and possible motives.

The lack of some representational body in the Church was noted by some respondents, and received strong endorsement from several who were no longer officially recognised as priests. For example:

"My major concern here is that the model of church government is like an eighteenth century autocracy... The Pope is all-powerful, and there are no constitutional checks or

balances to his power... Basically it's this upward centralisation that worries me greatly about the Church." (Resigned)

Others struggle with making a distinction between the Pope and the Curia. Thus one seminarian stated that he:

> "was not impressed by the isolated curia – too judgmental, too cold, too rigid. I'm not classing the Pope in this, though he is probably head of the Curia. Dialogue not condemnation is required. Bring them round by dialogue."

The last sentence seems to assume a manipulative idea of dialogue.

Those who saw the role of the Curia in terms of a longer clerical life experience, believed that it operated too closely on the model of a civil service or rigid bureaucracy.

> "I have no problem about the way the role of the Pope is functioning. The difficulty lies with the Roman Curia throughout its history. It functions too much like a civil service." (Non-parochial)

> "The Vatican is like haemophilia in the Royal Family. It's built into them. They cannot escape from the way they now think. It's full of diplomats and politicians." (Parish priest)

One important consequence of the perceived current style of governance is the dilution of the doctrine of collegiality.

> "One of the buzz terms of Vatican II was 'collegiality' with bishops as the representatives and leaders of the Roman churches. We have since witnessed, at the level of the international church, Rome removing or sacking bishops, or when an appointment came up, totally ignoring the façade of consultation within the diocese... (Resigned)

This criticism can take a more muted form amongst those who express concern about the adaptation of central edicts to local circumstances and the extent to which the Curia is knowledgeable about them.

> "What comes from Rome may not be entirely appropriate for

> each diocese. More localised areas would have to find a way forward, still obeying what Rome says but slightly interpreting it according to their own circumstances." (Seminarian)

> "Sometimes I wonder to what extent the Vatican does understand what is going on here... One of the things that would be very useful to us would be if some of the officials of the Roman Curia spent some time in Britain... and got a sense of what is really going on here... What does concern me sometimes is that some Catholics look upon the Vatican as the conservative repressive engine of the Church. And I don't see the Vatican that way at all... but sometimes they are so badly informed. (Bishop)

> "If these people in their offices in Rome every year had to spend two months actually working on the ground with people they'd be much the better for it." (Bishop)

Opinions on the reasons why the Vatican is adopting a more strict regime vary from a systematic attempt to withdraw from Vatican II to a simple but necessary correction of distortion.

> "The present Pope has tried to clamp down on freedoms and I'm convinced he's trying to restrict the movement that came from the Second Vatican Council. You can't even discuss things – the hierarchy in this country are petrified to talk about things.
> (Resigned)

A currently ministering parish priest expressed concern that unless Rome spoke out clearly the people would be dismayed and unity would not survive.

At the level of the diocese it would seem at first sight that those no longer in official ministry and those currently in office who express disappointment both criticise the role of local bishops. However, the former tend to the view that bishops fail to exercise their legitimate powers viz a viz the Curia, whilst the latter believe that bishops do not unambiguously support Rome. Such contrasting sources of criticism cannot make upholding unity an easy task.

> "Obedience seems to count more than truth... We have at present what I call a complicity of silence... Bishops don't dare

> speak out... I know many theologians who totally disagree but they disagree in private... So I think there is a kind of corruption happening." (Resigned)

> "The new catechism is not taken into account. Orders from Rome are ignored by the bishops. A bishop in England said that the document on collaborative ministry signed by sixteen cardinals and the Pope did not apply. Clearly it did. I came across teaching from the bishop against what is there in black and white. Another aspect is the teaching on social issues. The Common Good contains teachings that flatly contradict the teachings of the Pope, for example, how Catholics should deal with candidates (in an election) who vote for abortion... We know as priests that the Church is in a process of decline. Until recently the hierarchy pretended the opposite... The air of optimism of 'We are an Easter People' is not supported by the alarming rate of lapsation... I would like to see bishops publicly supporting the official teaching of the Church unambiguously and without fear of society." (Parish priest)

This parish priest was generally in support of what he termed a non-clericalist interpretation of collaboration on the grounds that *"the laity has access to areas the priest cannot get to"*. However, he also noted the difficulties raised in a parish by any strong grass roots protest.

> "... these people can often be very unrepresentative and can alienate other lay people because of their 'political agenda' and because a lot of lay people resent authority from other lay people compared to their docility if it is the decision of a celibate priest or nun."

Another point of systemic criticism is found in the observation of the ways in which governance can be overturned on the appointment of a new parish priest. As one respondent who longer ministers expressed it:

> "A priest gets a real community feeling going, produces all sorts of interesting changes, he is moved and another priest is appointed. According to church law, that priest can do what he likes, overturn all and carry on as if it never happened. That is unacceptable... We've almost got a fascist-type government."

the appointment of a new parish priest

Similar change may occur at diocesan level, of course, and will continue until we find a mechanism for the development and ownership of policy which is not based on a monarchical principle.

Conclusion

In terms of Canon Law the priestly role in the governance of the Church seems to be clearly defined. This is not the case in relation to the role of lay people. It is perhaps optimistic to expect in the near future any revision in the Canon Law, in view of the tendency of recent changes towards a tightening of clerical control, and the satisfaction amongst priests with the general level of lay participation already achieved as a result of 'delegation' from the clergy and the acceptance by lay people of 'churchy' roles in a marginal capacity. Those no longer in active ministry are less satisfied with the levels of lay participation, and many refer politely to 'the distance' of the Curia from real life. In discussions of governance the anxiety over potential threats to unity is evident. So is an alarm about what people would actually make of discrimination in Church Teaching: *"If we water down the teaching, people will see disunity and disharmony, and quickly leave"*. Yet the Church should not be viewed simply as a political party in which perceived lack of unity is the kiss of death. We need in fact much more work on the Church as polity. (Cornwell, 1999)

Chapter Five

PRIESTLY AND LAY AUTHORITY

THIS CHAPTER CONSIDERS four topics: attitudes to the distribution of authority in the Roman Catholic Church; the distinctive nature of clerical authority; the authentic role of the laity; and the legitimate power that can be exercised by women.

The distribution of authority

As can be seen from Table Three participants were generally satisfied that priests, the Pope, the College of Cardinals, the diocesan Bishop, heads of diocesan departments, Cardinal Hume and Cardinal Winning exercised the right amount of authority. Although approximately half the respondents believed that the Heads of Curial Congregations and the Curial officials exercised the right amount of authority, a similar proportion of participants believed that they exercised too much. Some drew attention to what they saw as authoritarian attitudes and a lack of trust by the Curia in local bishops, both individually and as Conferences. As one bishop suggested:

> *"I think much of their authority could be delegated to the Bishop's Conference."*

This assumes that what is **delegated** does not already belong in principle to the head of the local Church.

The majority of respondents believed that lay people exercised too little authority. An analysis of the taped interviews suggests, however, caution in interpreting the simple judgements of too little, too much, and so on. Sometimes the comments made suggest that what respondents have in mind is registering support or appraisal. For example, Cardinal Hume could be regarded as 'a good thing' and yet attention would not be paid to the authority he actually exercised. Again, respondents wanted to make some distinction in relation to the objects towards which authority might be exercised. So, bishops might be seen as exercising too much authority 'on their own patch' and too little in relation to central institutions in Rome.

lay people exercised too little authority

TABLE THREE
Exercising Authority in the Church

	Too little	Right amount	Too much	Don't know/ Not applicable
College of Bishops	19	31	12	3
Heads of diocesan departments	6	36	14	9
Curial officials	3	30	24	8
Cardinal Hume (Scotland: Cardinal Winning)	10	48	4	3
Lay people	51	9	–	5
Heads of Curial Congregations	4	23	31	7
You as a priest	3	31	18	13
The Pope	1	41	21	2
The College of Cardinals	8	35	15	7
Your diocesan Bishop	6	40	16	3

Clerical authority

Participants were asked about the authority they would claim that could not or should not be claimed by a lay person. The vast majority clearly distinguished between the authority that they would claim, and that which they believed belonged to a lay person. First and foremost, respondents believed that ordination confers authority, from Christ, upon the priest. This enables the priest to administer the sacraments and to preach. In particular respondents referred to celebrating Mass, hearing confession and the authority to absolve from sin:

> "Only the priests can celebrate the sacraments. I don't seek to differentiate between common priesthood and the ministerial priesthood, but I believe the ministerial priest has a function in

ordination confers authority

> *the church and has a God-given gift to use it."* (Recently ordained)

> *"To celebrate the sacraments, that would be my benchmark for the authority of the priests."* (Parish priest)

These same respondents believed that the lay person does not have the authority to claim what are believed to be priestly functions, for example no participant felt it was appropriate for the lay person to celebrate Mass (although they could conduct a eucharistic service), or to absolve sin. Other areas, such as preaching, were also contentious amongst participants. Some felt their theological training meant they alone have the appropriate knowledge to preach the Gospel. Others believed that a lay person could preach in church on certain occasions. Several participants mentioned that lay people act as prayer group leaders, or as spiritual directors. Participants also reported that lay people help to run parishes and encourage greater co-operation between the laity and the clergy:

> *"They can be spiritual directors, prayer leaders. They can do absolutely everything by right of their baptism."* (Parish priest)

> *"The way things are going now, the authority a lay person couldn't claim is the authority of the priest himself. Lay people do work as eucharistic ministers."* (Seminarian)

The notion of the authority of the priest himself may sit uncomfortably with a baptismal source of authority. It may also be contested in terms of early church practice (see Lawrence in Hoose ed. forthcoming) and a legitimacy that is earned rather than God-given.

legitimacy is earned

> *"Theoretically, I have no authority. But one needs to build in the fact that we are a community. An awful lot of people would say a lay person couldn't celebrate Mass... Who celebrated Mass in the early church? Presumably it was whoever ran the house, presided at the meal."* (Resigned)

> *"I don't think there's a source of authority apart from what the people attribute to him or her, and from the innate good quality of their message and leadership and personal advantage. I think in the end authority comes down to the example of the person holding it."* (Resigned)

Belief in a divine source of priestly authority can encourage an attitude of superiority implicit perhaps in the disdainful comment of one seminarian.

> *"Joe Catholic has not been given that [sacramental] authority to hear confession for example."*

The exclusive authority claimed by priests also encompasses the definition of orthodoxy.

> *"Administering the sacraments, interpretation of Scripture and the interpretation of moral and ethical behaviour. Although we have consciences, it is not up to the individual to decide. The Church tells us what is what, and how the Church believes that God has spoken."* (Recently ordained)

authentic teaching

The authority to decide authentic teaching is, of course, most evident in the responses of the bishops who participated in the study.

> *"I have the authority to decide what is authentic and what is truly conducive to the growth of the Church in the name of the Church... My authority is needed to make an act of the Church... only a Bishop can give authority that something is an authentic act of the Church..."* (Bishop)

> *"Well, a lay person should not claim to decide what is true or false in the faith. They would decide by their own conscience... Personal faith differs much more than people realise, but as to what is the faith of the Church, no one lay person can have a decisive voice... Locally that would be my responsibility, but a priest must work in harmony with his fellow priests and his Bishop, and the Bishop should work in harmony with his fellow Bishops... Christ organised it as a top down structure."* (Bishop)

> *"I have got roles or responsibilities in liturgy and teaching that lay people don't have... Also celebrating Mass as a priest... We all celebrate Mass but it's the priest alone who has got certain ministries in the celebration of Mass that lay people don't have, likewise in some of the sacraments, although not in all of them... I also have got a responsibility for ensuring that the Christian faith is taught and is taught without error in the*

diocese and that is a personal responsibility that I have, and it's a devolved responsibility to the priest and the parish." (Bishop)

Two aspects invite comment. First, the responses appear to ignore the fruits of an historical and developing notion of church teaching. Ideas of the sealed deposit of faith should be tested against Lonergan's distinction (1972) between dogmatic theology and doctrinal theology. The former *"is classicist. It tends to take it for granted that on each issue there is one and only one true proposition… In contrast, doctrinal theology is historically minded. It knows that the meaning of a proposition becomes determinate only within a context. It knows that contexts vary with the varying brands of common sense, with the evolution of cultures, with the differentiations of human consciousness, and with the presence or absence of intellectual, moral and religious conversion"*. (p. 333)

Second, the idea of a teaching church should be judged against an adequate idea of teaching and of learning. One may accept teachers as authorities, but this is different from accepting still less obeying their teaching. *"Teaching is not taming, ruling, restoring to health, conditioning, or commanding, because none of these activities is possible in relation to a pupil."* (Oakeshott, 1989 p. 44)

Authentic role of the laity

Many participants were happy for lay people to take on a wide variety of roles, apart from sacramental functions. Many mentioned that the management of the parish was important for the laity. Roles included running committees, administration, bookkeeping, leading prayer groups, participation in liturgy, implementing parish catechetical programmes and exercising leadership.

> *"They could be the leader or the guide within the parish, the animator in a particular area."* (Parish priest)

> *"They can be lots of things from eucharistic ministers to bookkeepers, in the parish, they can be involved with maintenance."*
> (Seminarian)

> *"90% of my work as a fulltime chaplain could be done by anybody. I'd have to celebrate the sacraments. People have to be*

management of the parish

> *involved and take over the priest's role in a sense e.g. parishioners can visit other parishioners. The priest isn't exclusively the Church in his parish, he is part of the Church, primarily a servant, not a school teacher with a big stick."*
>
> (Parish priest)

> *"[The laity can exercise] roles of leadership in the wider sense of the word. If you assume that a Church is a community and a network of small communities, anything which will build up community is an authentic role of leadership."* (Resigned)

> *"It would be very much the roles to do with parish life – education, catechesis, liturgy, helping to lead the congregation in worship, parish council work alongside the priest in a day-to-day management of the parish. I'd like to see the priest and the laity together having open administration of finances, but the parish priest has the responsibility and therefore the authority to manage them."* (Seminarian)

Lay people could take on a pastoral role in conjunction with the priest, and indeed support and assist the priest in parish life. Participants reported they needed help with management, advice and decision making:

> *"There are many, many roles of practical management, financial management, building management, organisational management... they have a great deal to contribute, but trying to preserve the unity of the church in a community of love, it has to be ultimately in union with a priest."* (Bishop)

> *"The [laity have the] role of support and advice and count in decision."* (Resigned)

Many participants were aware of a new situation, in so far as lay people in their parish were often professionals or experts in various fields. They hoped to integrate their expertise and practical skills into the running of the parish.

> *"Lay people who are experts in so many fields will have a voice on commissions – help bishops in their teaching authority e.g. medical science. Bishops do need to listen to the experts. But those experts are not teachers; they do not have the authority of the ordained hierarchy."* (Parish priest)

> *"There are practical tasks that ordinary people, lay or clerical, can do. They are infinite e.g. skills in accountancy, education, nursing, medical work, charity, prison visiting."* (Resigned)

Some participants also pointed out that it was important to have lay participation in order to spread the Gospel and furthermore to put the Gospel into practice.

to spread the gospel

> *"The Church is there to proclaim the Gospel and build up the body of Christ. Lay people participate in that mission by being witness to the faith in their own lives, taking part in worship and communicating the faith... The clergy are there to spread the faith. It's the laity who are best placed to be missionary agents."* (Parish priest)

In order to conceptualise the role of lay people in the thinking of ordained ministers, participants were presented with five statements regarding the role of lay people (Doohan 1984 Ch.1). They were asked to indicate the extent to which they agreed or disagreed with each statement using a scale of 1-10, where 1 = completely disagree, and 10 = fully agree.

The five statements were:

1. Jesus entrusted the mission of the Church to bishops and priests. The laity's role is to support and **assist** them.

2. The role of lay Christians is to act as a bridge between Christ's Church and the world, to be a **sign** of God's love in the world.

3. Lay people are called to **transform the world**, make it good: to heal it of sin, develop and prepare it for Christ's second coming.

4. Lay people are **partners** with the hierarchy in the mission of the church and should participate with them in teaching, ministry and church administration.

5. Lay people do not have a role in the church. **They are the church!** The question is, rather, what is the special role of the ordained minister.

The results, averaged out, are presented in Table Four.

TABLE FOUR
Role of lay people in the Church

Statement number	Average score
Statement 1	4.5
Statement 2	7.5
Statement 3	8.4
Statement 4	8.2
Statement 5	6.8

Statements 3 and 4 were the most popular and were very close in their average scores, followed by statement 2, then statement 5. Statement 1 was the one participants least agreed with.

Statement 1 received low scores from a number of participants who did not agree that Jesus directly entrusted the mission of the Church to bishops and priests. They felt that it was historically inaccurate to suggest that the Church in this form was established by Jesus. These respondents also disliked the use of the word 'assist' for the laity – they felt that the laity's role was greater than this.

Statement 2 generally met with agreement, but some participants expressed reservations about the description of lay Christians as a *"bridge"* between Christ's Church and the world. There was broad agreement over the role of lay people as a 'sign' of God's love in the world.

Statement 3 was the most popular with participants, although a number commented that **all** Christians, not just lay people, are called in the way described by this statement.

Statement 4 was liked by participants, and generated the least number of criticisms. The collaborative theme of this statement appeared to be its main attraction. However, participants differed in the extent to which they felt lay people should be involved in the ministries described in this statement.

Statement 5 received lower scores from some participants because they felt the statement did not take into account the role of the ordained priesthood in the Church. These participants felt the statement should describe the Church as **both** lay people and ordained priesthood.

Participation of lay people in selection and in appointments

Participants were asked if lay people should participate more fully in the following:

- the selection of candidates for the priesthood
- the appointment of priests
- the appointment of bishops

Many participants reported that the lay people were already involved in the selection of candidates for priesthood and this included the laity who might originally encourage someone to joint the priesthood:

> *"Lay experts should be involved to say whether a candidate has the human qualities to be a priest. Laity are consulted when candidates spend time in a parish."* (Recently ordained)

> *"I think now there would be one or two lay people on the panel. That's not a bad thing, because they can have different questions. They'd be more interested in asking, 'What would you see as the role of the laity in the church?' because that would affect them. A priest might not ask them that."* (Recently ordained)

> *"Already the laity have a big role. The Church knows it needs lay people with common sense, as well as priests to judge on suitability."* (Recently ordained)

> *"At least two of the three interviews I had were with lay people and they had a big say."* (Seminarian)

> *"... all candidates are seen by two priests and about four lay people at the early stage, they then go through a selection process which is partly priests and partly professional lay people of one sort or another... so there's a fair amount of lay participation."* (Bishop)

Other respondents felt it would be positive to include the laity in this process as they were most likely to know the needs of their own parish.

> *"It wouldn't be a bad thing because there are very astute people*

the needs of their own parish

who are not necessarily ordained who can see why a person would be suitable." (Recently ordained)

"I'd like to see some more ordinary people selecting candidates — sometimes we have people who have an agenda or who come from an extreme position within the church and they are highly educated — it would be great to just have someone who is someone's mum, or someone who goes to Mass on a Sunday and tries their best and knows the qualities — not just priestly ones, but human ones. People who are down to earth — they're the ones you are going to spend most time with when you're a priest. You aren't going to spend much time with other priests." (Seminarian)

"Yes, [the laity] should be involved because ultimately you are going to serve them. You need to have a section of lay people competent to evaluate candidates as they come along."

(Recently ordained)

lay involvement inappropriate

A very small number of participants did not feel it was appropriate for the laity to be involved or believed that their involvement should be limited.

"It's like asking if non-accountants should have a greater role in the selection of candidates for accountancy… There are so many things connected with living the priestly life and preparing for it that priests understand. I'm not saying that lay people don't understand that but they would have to be very exceptional lay people to empathise with that, whereas you don't have to be a very exceptional priest to know it by experience. I think in so far as part of being a priest is being professional, then like any profession or trade the people principally associated with it should have the say in that and not people from outside." (Parish priest)

"I don't think the laity can be involved — what would they know about me? It's not practical." (Non-parochial)

"I don't think if would be of benefit. It begs another question: Is there a problem in the way we are choosing our candidates? And I don't really think there is." (Recently ordained priest)

The 1993 American survey found that only 25% of priests thought it a good idea for parishes to choose their own priests, but 50% favoured priests *"choosing their own bishop"*.

The current system of appointment of parish priests by the bishop was considered by many participants to be the most appropriate method. Some were concerned that the laity would only choose the most popular priests for their parish, and not necessarily the best person for its needs. A small number were also concerned that priests would begin applying for 'parish posts', rather than being sent to the parish which might need them the most, assuming, of course, that bishops can both assess and respond appropriately to need.

Bishops should appoint parish priests

> *"We trust to providence that the Church in wisdom is sending priests to a place where they don't know who they are getting. If everyone starts fighting over it, 'Oh we want Father so-and-so because he is a good laugh', it's not real.* (Seminarian)

> *"The priest has been appointed by the bishop. I know in the Church of England they have that model… That's just not for the Catholic Church. You're just told where you're going, but I think that's much closer to the time of Jesus… People don't know what they are getting but that's not a bad thing, a priest can be different to the people he's going to serve and that enriches a community."* (Recently ordained priest)

> *"I think the Bishop should be able to appoint a priest. Again the bishop should take advice when filling a particular parish. If you leave it to the lay people you might get a position where priests apply for posts."* (Parish priest)

> *"No, [the laity should not appoint priests] because some priests are very popular and some priests aren't. It would be uncharitable and unkind for one priest to be asked to do everything while others stood on the touchlines."* (Recently ordained priest)

Furthermore, a few participants felt the laity were unlikely to know much about the candidate, his experience or his abilities, so would not be in a position to make an informed decision.

> *"With the appointment of priests, most Catholics would not want to be involved. How would they know anything about this person?* (Non-parochial)

One of the bishops was very aware that time constraints meant there was often little time to consult other members of the church or laity regarding appointments.

> *"If it's possible, in an ideal world it would be wonderful, but often time is against you, and often they are going to ask you for someone that ten other parishes have asked for as well... I think any consultation has to be prefaced by the remark, 'Well we've got a limited pool and in the end they may not be able to match your expectations with the reality.'"* (Bishop)

consultation with the laity

However, many respondents were in favour of some form of consultation with the laity, and a very small number, mainly those priests resigned from active ministry, felt the laity should approve the appointment of a candidate:

> *"There is a committee that looks at appointments – representatives of areas of the diocese meet the vicar general and discuss appointments. They could get some views of lay people and consider them prior to appointments."* (Recently ordained priest)

> *"Theoretically they do [already]. [Candidates] are presented to the laity for approval. There should be much greater psychological input, screening and have lay participation in that."* (Parish priest)

> *"I think [the laity] should be heard – it's what the parish needs. We wrote to the Bishop once to say 'This is what our parish is like... There are loads of families. We don't want somebody put out to grass to retire', and then we get another 68 year old recovering from a heart attack!* (Resigned)

> *"Of course they should, there's no reason why not. They don't have the same kind of options available to them because there aren't a hundred applicants for every post, so Bishop's problems in moving priests around are there to be seen, and sometimes they are very confidential... he may have a special knowledge about it."* (Resigned)

Views on the appointment of bishops were very similar to those regarding the appointment of priests, that is they were largely in favour of some form of lay participation in the appointment of bishops. The bishops in the study mentioned that lay people were involved with the appointments of bishops.

> *"If the bishop is for the people, they should have a say. The bishop is for everybody – priests and people. He's the representative of Christ in the diocese."* (Seminarian)

> *"Again, lay people have the opportunity to participate, for example Cardinal Hume was very much a lay appointment..."* (Bishop)

> *"So I know that lay people are consulted... but it's the secrecy of the thing... This obsession with secrecy I don't understand it...I think it's too secret.* (Bishop)

The participatory role of women

Participants were asked if they were in favour of women in key decision making roles in the church. The examples used were:

- Nuns or lay women as Heads of Vatican Congregations
- Women as judges in marriage tribunals
- Women involved in the appointment of priests and bishops

The majority of participants were very much in favour of women in these positions and furthermore felt that a 'female perspective' would be a positive advantage. Some made the qualification that the women should be competent, and familiar with appropriate church teachings, and with relevant aspects of Canon Law. Others reported that women were already involved in some or all of these positions.

a 'female' perspective

> *"I wouldn't make any distinction between women and men. I think the competence and knowledge and devotion and spirituality is the key factor, sexuality is not relevant."* (Resigned)

> *"I know women are used widely as assessors in Canon Law cases. I see no fundamental reason why not; law is law, it's an objective judgement of fact so it doesn't matter if a man or woman is involved as long as they are qualified."* (Parish priest)

> *[Appointment of bishops and priests] "There you are actually verging on the hierarchy set out by Christ, so they can't actually*

make the decisions, but they can certainly advise... We do consult women in selecting candidates." (Bishop)

Two priests mentioned there might be cultural problems involved in the inclusion of women in these positions.

"The Catholic Church is very much a male church in its hierarchical structures because women are not ordained. In theory there's no problem with lay women as Heads of Vatican departments, but I think it is a long way off. We are still in the structure of all male celibates... I wouldn't have a problem with lay women or men as Heads of Vatican congregations, but the structures have been in place for centuries." (Recently ordained)

[Nuns/women as heads of Vatican Congregations] "We've had them as heads of other things and it hasn't worked well. The problem is the training. The church doesn't run as a business. It runs a lot on tradition. You can't run a parish as you run a business, it's not like running a school." (Non-parochial)

Conclusion

sources of legitimacy

In this chapter we have turned from the exercise of governance to the sources of its legitimacy. These are to be found in different views on the history of the Church. On the one hand, respondents argue that not only did Christ knowingly found a Church but that it had a particular structure, that of a top-down organisation. On the other hand, it is argued that the early Christians developed a variety of practices concerning the roles of what became those of priesthood and of the laity.

The appropriate roles of lay people based on their expertise are acknowledged, but *"experts are not teachers"*. Teachers, of course, should be experts. Moreover, this bounded view of the limits of expertise seems echoed in the distinction some wish to make between celebrating the sacraments and other aspects of a priest's work.

The five statements presented to respondents describing different views of the proper role of the laity in the Church divided respondents into those who confidently rejected one and accepted another and those who saw merit in more than one. This suggests that further work is required into attempts to characterise the precise role of lay people in terms of assistance, sign, transformation, participation and the bewildering idea of corporate personality. According to this last notion the identity of a group is in some way embodied in one individual (Pope, bishop or priest), so that members of the group somehow come to recognise themselves in this single, if not singular, individual.

Chapter Six

CONTROVERSIAL ISSUES FACING THE CHURCH

IN AN EARLIER CHAPTER we described the priests' views of the main problems facing the contemporary Church. No one mentioned the doctrinal issues the research selected for discussion. Respondents were shown a card listing some of the controversial issues facing the Roman Catholic Church today:

Celibacy
Offering communion to Christians of other denominations
Women priests
Contraception
The validity of Anglican orders
Married priests
Sacramental participation of the divorced

Interviewers carefully reminded respondents that they should only give their views on current Church teaching where they were willing to discuss the issues. This approach was adopted because of sensitivity to the fact that 'women priests' was included as one of the subjects. In the event, only one respondent (a seminarian) did not wish to discuss the issues raised.

Some of the issues may possess greater resonance for the day-to-day lives of Catholics than others. Contraception may have greater significance than the validity of Anglican Orders, and women priests and married priests may achieve indirect importance in the light of the downturn in vocations. However, all the issues share a common characteristic: they have been the subject of definitive pronouncement at the central or local level. The papal decree condemning Anglican Orders is the oldest of the positions to be defined, but it was used recently by Cardinal Ratzinger as an example of magisterial teaching. In relation to each of these issues three attitudes predominate: enthusiastic endorsement, acceptance, and allowing for some possibility of change, though without articulating any theory of doctrinal development. Each of the issues will now be separately considered.

the spirituality of Christ

Celibacy

One of the seminarians, perhaps mildly critical of the research interest in this issue, responded:

> *"People who meet you are fixated with this issue. It's the first, the last, the only thing people latch onto."*

He continued with a strong defence of celibacy linked to the spirituality of Christ, as a symbol and as a renunciation of sexual power.

> *"For those who feel celibacy can be lived with, it can be an important witness within the Church. It's not for the sake of an ecclesiastical rule. Celibacy is based on the spirituality of Christ, and the identity of the priest is grounded in that. Celibacy does not take precedence over married life, but it is distinct and can witness to a different life style. Celibacy is not unnatural but has to be linked to wider aspects of the ministry. It is a symbol of single-mindedness. A form of impartial relationship that does not use sexual power. In the priest sexual power is integrated, rechanneled. Mutual love and celibate love are not that far from one another, because they are essentially placed in the service of other people."*

This is an unusually elaborated celebration of celibacy. Others who support the practice rely on the sacramental identity with Christ and the essential place of the sign of celibacy in the priesthood.

> *"It's an essential sign, springing from the nature of the Church, that in today's secular society is even more necessary than in the past. My understanding of it is that it is not essential in the sense of the hierarchical structure of the Church, but is something very close to the Gospel."* (Bishop)

> *"I'm wholly in favour of the celibacy of the clergy... it's an imitation of Jesus Christ and I would consider it a great sign to the world that the priest is someone who has devoted himself entirely to the service of the Church. I think it would be a great tragedy if it were to change in a fundamental way as the norm. I couldn't do what I do if I were married. All this about getting more priests if we got rid of celibacy is a lot of nonsense."*
>
> (Parish priest)

Celibacy can also be supported as a sign of identification with those marginalised by society and of the fact that priests are prepared to suffer hardship. Yet there is also some concern that the extent of the hardship is not recognised and is not a topic for open discussion.

identification with those marginalised

> "It affects you in different ways. When you haven't got someone to love any more. I miss getting hugs, which I used to from my family. Sometimes it will be sexual, which is a real loss, sometimes just wanting to kiss someone or hug someone or just hold someone. The great loss is talking to a woman at that level." (Seminarian)

> "You have to have someone prepared to discuss it without hiding. To say 'God created you for procreation' that's the starting point. They have to admit that, and within that, celibacy is a choice we have made, and you have to understand that you are going to have sexual desires and be attractive to the opposite sex... You have to get them to understand that you have to live with the struggle of your sexual desires for as long as you are a priest, and that you can never be in control of it... If celibacy was discussed thoroughly by a very good psychologist in the first year at seminary, then I think you will get people who really understand what celibacy means." (Recently ordained)

There was general agreement amongst respondents that celibacy was not necessarily connected to cases of child abuse, but little realisation of the effects of revelations of child abuse by priests beyond the creation of a scandal. Fr. O'Keefe believes that *"One of the effects on whole communities is that suddenly there's a 'sexualisation' of the priest. Until then it never occurred to people to imagine a priest being involved in sexual activity"*. (Butler ed. 1999, p.80)

Those accepting celibacy without enthusiasm are to be found amongst the seminarians:

celibacy without enthusiasm

> "It's unnatural which is quite obvious but you have to accept the issue in order to be in the ministerial priesthood. Sometimes I agree with it, sometimes not.... As a married priest you would be living in a minute community and that community becomes more important." (Seminarian)

> *"Celibacy comes with the package of priesthood. You don't join the Church to change the rules, you join it for what it is."*
>
> (Seminarian)

a single minded service

One way in which recent experience in the church can be used to test celibacy as enabling a single minded service of the parish is to be found in the lives of ordained former Anglican clergy. One of these commented:

> *"The argument of the Church is that you cannot serve God and a wife and family and my answer to that is 'Rubbish, of course you can'. My family understand that I have a life of shifting priorities, and that there are times when they are supremely important in my life and they come first, and there are other moments when they acknowledge that the Church comes first, corporately and also its individual members. And if there's a family gathering here and the telephone rings and somebody needs me because they need their priest I go. And I understand that and my parish understands that and my family understands that. Obviously I've got many friends as well as colleagues who are celibate priests and I look at their lifestyles and frankly I don't see any difference. They also have their friends and their social aspects and these could be stumbling blocks in the same way that marriage could be seen as a stumbling block... The Orthodox Churches of the East still have married priests – a very large number of them – not bishops admittedly, but priests. And there is no difficulty. And I think without any shadow of doubt if only the Catholic Church could actually come to grips and bite the bullet on this particular issue, the problem with vocations would by and large be solved."* (Recently ordained)

the element of compulsion

The possibility of change in the celibacy rule and of questioning celibacy as an essential sign is suggested in different ways. Some argue against the element of compulsion.

> *"If the Church really believes in celibacy, it doesn't have to impose it, there are enough people who would choose it."* (Non-parochial)

> *"I think celibacy for some people is a noble calling, but I do not think it should be a compulsory part of the priesthood."*
>
> (Resigned)

This view is echoed by those envisaging the possibility of the co-existence of celibate and of married priests.

> *"I suspect there should be real consideration given to the idea of ordaining what they call mature married men..."* (Bishop)

> *"I think the important thing about celibacy is that it should be a genuine free commitment. If it is merely a package deal, it can be harmful... we have to recognise that the Eastern Church have had a married and celibate clergy parallel all the time..."*
> (Bishop)

Finally, one bishop considered the very serious, global effects of the celibacy rule:

> *"I think it's a great gift to the Church. Having said that, my caveat is, is it right to place the requirement of celibacy over and above the fact that many, many people of the Church in the world are effectively denied the Eucharist because of celibacy?"*

Married priests

As will be seen from the list reproduced above, several other issues of concern to the Roman Catholic Church were discussed following the issue of celibacy, before respondents returned to the related question of married priests. The two subjects were intentionally divided in the interview.

When the subject of married priests was discussed, a large majority (75%) of respondents was not only open to the possibility of married priests in the Roman Catholic Church, but actively in favour of allowing a **choice** between celibacy and marriage. Only among seminarians were respondents divided equally as to whether priests should be allowed to marry or not. In all other categories there was a majority in favour of change. Priests who have resigned their active ministries (many of whom are now married) were unanimously in favour of married priests.

The research suggests that when discussing celibacy, respondents were relating the discussion to themselves, and defending – or re-committing themselves to – their own decision to remain celibate. When the discussion moved away from celibacy to married priests,

a choice between celibacy and marriage

respondents seemed able to distance the discussion from themselves, and perhaps felt more able to comment freely.

> *"We've got married priests. I can see that happening a great deal more. In this day and age, a man can retire at 50 and have a practical life of 20 years- he doesn't have the responsibility of bringing up children."* (Parish priest)

> *"I have got some very good friends who are married priests. No problem at all."* (Parish priest)

> *"I have no difficulty there. Married people can have a desire for ministry as great as mine. There is room for the married and the unmarried."* (Parish priest)

> *"I see no objection to having married priests in principle. I think there will always be a tremendous preference for celibate priests."* (Bishop)

Some, but by no means all, respondents made a distinction between being allowed to marry **prior** to ordination (which they would be happy with), and being allowed to marry **after** ordination (with which they would not be so happy).

> *"It [celibacy] ought to be voluntary. I'd rather see the Orthodox way of doing it – you choose before ordination to get married or no, and after ordination you can't then marry. I think it's a very wise situation – monks and bishops remain celibate, priests who are working every day in the parish, they don't have to be."* (Recently ordained)

the admission of married former Anglican clergy

There is no question that the admission of married former Anglican clergy to the Roman Catholic priesthood has had a significant impact. Some respondents almost felt they could not argue with the principle of married priests, given that they were now working alongside them. Some, perhaps inevitably, were angered by the fact that former Anglicans could be married priests, while long-serving and devoted Catholic priests were forced to leave in order to be married.

> *"I got angry about the recent decision to ordain former Anglican clergy who were married, because I knew a couple of*

clergy who had left the Catholic priesthood to get married, and they would never be allowed to be priests." (Recently ordained)

"Ex-Anglicans are converting and becoming priests. That causes problems for Catholic priests who have left the ministry to get married. It's the major problem for the Church in England – we have to decide where we stand. At the moment, I'd still choose celibacy, but I don't think there's a problem with married priesthood." (Seminarian)

Some of the respondents taking part in the study were themselves priests who had resigned their active ministries in order to marry. It is not surprising that some of them found the current situation "bizarre":

"There are married priests. What's the problem? The bizarre thing is that there are married priests, but people like me are kept out." (Resigned – married)

"I know that there are many married priests who would be willing and prepared to come back to minister in some way or another. But there are those, of course, who have been hurt and offended and who would never set foot near a church again."
(Resigned)

"I hoped that I would be back in the priesthood again before I died. I think it's the only solution. I think we should have both (married and celibate priests). I think marriage is part of growth – it's part of normal human development." (Resigned)

"So many people have left because of the Church's intransigence on this matter. For most people it is irrelevant if priests are married. Most people I know think that if a priest was married he would have an all-round experience, he would have more to give." (Resigned)

The small numbers who were opposed to the idea of married priests becoming an option tended to refer to the practical difficulties they foresaw, or to the special circumstances surrounding the Anglican clergy who have recently been ordained in the Catholic Church:

107

> *"Theologically it's not a problem, but practically it might be – how do you support the family, how can a priest be devoted to his family and his work as a priest? It would take an exceptional man to do it well."* (Recently ordained)

> *"A priest can never marry but we do have dispensations allowing married people to become priests. The Church is being sensitive to former Anglicans who are married and who are called to be priests. It is rubbish to suggest that marriage is a solution to the problems of fewer men entering the priesthood. It's the Gospel tradition to leave everything to follow Christ."*
> (Recently ordained)

Offering communion to Christians of other denominations

At the time this research was being conducted, the issue of offering communion to Christians of another denomination coincided with the publication of the English and Welsh Bishops' document *One Bread One Body*. Briefly, the first part of this document sets out the Church's theological understanding of the Eucharist, while the second part explains what some respondents referred to as the *"rules and regulations"* (in fact the Norms) in terms of receiving communion.

Once again, those who have resigned their active ministry make a difference to the *overall* view. Virtually all of these respondents wished to see a change which would allow Christians of other denominations to take communion more freely with their Catholic brothers and sisters. If these respondents are excluded, the position changes: three quarters of seminarians, the newly ordained, parochial and non-parochial clergy, and Bishops are happy with the status quo, with only about a quarter wishing to see change.

happy with the status quo

Many respondents referred to *One Bread One Body* in the course of the discussion, although not all appeared to have read it, and not all respondents were clear about the Church's current practice. For example, as we shall see some appeared to believe that it is *never* possible to offer communion to Christians of other denominations, and some stated that they would refuse to do this themselves.

This was one of the issues that did not attract simple acceptance though one respondent considered it a practical problem. For the rest in the words of one seminarian, it is difficult to appreciate how dear the Eucharist is to Roman Catholics. It is also difficult to overestimate its distinctiveness.

> *"Open communion for anyone who is baptised is a misunderstanding of the nature of the Church and the nature of communion. Communion is an initiation into the mystery of the Church."* (Parish priest)

> *"This comes down to our belief in the Eucharist which is the one thing that distinguishes the Catholic Church, belief in the real presence... Catholics believe that the Eucharist is the actual body and blood of Christ."* (Parish priest)

Any broadening of the official guidelines through the unilateral action of a priest,

> *"Does a great disservice to the people who are offered communion because it means that there is no particular reason to become a Catholic. If we believe that being Catholic is important then we don't want to put obstacles in people's way, and by giving communion liberally there's no reason for someone to convert, or less reason than if we adhere to the rule as it is."* (Parish priest)

Those respondents in favour of the status quo tended to state that they believed that Christians should not receive communion together until full unity has been achieved. Such communion is not to be regarded as a fruitful means to unity.

> *"Communion is offered to Christians of another denomination only in what you might call 'emergency' circumstances, and then only to Christians who hold the same view of the Eucharist – for instance the Orthodox or certain Anglicans. It should not be the norm that other churches can simply receive communion in our churches, or Catholics in other churches, because the taking of communion is a public affirmation that there is already a communion of faith, and if that is not so, then it is improper to do it. Since we are not in perfect communion of faith, it should not be the norm."* (Parish priest)

> *"I don't think it should be done. It's deceptive. To offer communion when there's not communion there is pointless."*
> (Recently ordained)

Others talk of this possibility as unjust, as betrayal and hypocritical.

> *"Inter-communion with Anglicans and Protestants – I'd agree with the Church's stance – taking communion is symbolic of a wider communion between the Churches, and if there isn't full communion in faith or a shared sacramental understanding, then inter-communion is inappropriate."* (Seminarian)

Those who recognise the pain of Christian disunity are nonetheless sure of the reasons for the Church's teaching, and also express some anxiety about the dilution of that teaching.

> *"We all believe different things about the Eucharist. Catholic tradition is that by receiving the Eucharist we become one because of the doctrine of transubstantiation. Other Christians don't believe that. It seems selfish and hard not to share Communion, but the Church has good theological reasons."*
> (Recently ordained)

> *"Very few denominations hold the same belief in the real blood and body of Christ. It's difficult and upsetting that other people feel excluded, but I think it's right as we stand. The Catholic Church has to hold to her principles. I'm not happy with the situation because I'm sad we are separated, but it's important the Church doesn't lay down its principles just because everyone else is upset about it."* (Seminarian)

'Upset' does perhaps less than justice to the experience of one non-parochial priest.

> *"I work with ministers of other denominations. At Christmas Eve Mass, my fellow Anglican chaplain sat at the back – I was sad that we couldn't have done Mass together whereas we did almost everything else in the work of the chaplaincy together."*

Nor does it express adequately the disunity experienced by those marrying across denominational boundaries:

> "In situations like a mixed marriage, it seems stupid when we stress the unity of the couple, if they decide to have a Nuptial Mass, one receives communion and one receives a blessing. I think if the person respects the belief of the Catholic Church on the real presence, it should be allowed." (Recently ordained)

The bishops all voiced support for *One Bread One Body*. One commented that it was intended as a theology of the Eucharist, but people simply ignored the first part, and went immediately to the rules and regulations.

The publication was valued by the bishops as presenting a balance between two senses of communion: as a reality for those celebrating the Mass and as a sign of being in communion with other bishops and the Bishop of Rome. Most, however, recognised the pastoral difficulties and did not believe it was the last word.

> "I think we've got it just about right at the moment. There's a balance to be struck between communion as a sign of communion with those who are receiving the Lord with you. As I understand it those who receive communion at a Mass I am celebrating are in full communion with me, and I am in full communion with the Bishop of Rome, and other Bishops all over the world. Now if they're not in communion with me, or if they're not in communion with the Pope... in the same way I think they shouldn't receive communion at the Catholic service. As you know the Guidelines at the moment do say there are certain circumstances where non-Catholics can receive communion at a Catholic service. And while that does present certain pastoral difficulties, it's good to know that that can happen in certain circumstances – interchurch families mainly." (Bishop)

Two bishops hoped for more sharing in the future, and saw the issue as very much still open to debate. *One Bread One Body* for them was *"not the last word"*:

more sharing in the future

> "I suppose that the basic theology of the Catholic Church is that sharing communion is an expression of unity, rather than a means to unity. And I find that slightly difficult to square with some of the prayers in the liturgy, because the prayers in the liturgy not only speak of communion as an expression of

unity but as a means to unity, and I don't think you can have it both ways... I think it was an attempt to see where we are at present... it's good theology at the beginning. I certainly don't believe that Holy Communion should be open to just anybody, but maybe there are other areas in which intercommunion or sharing communion should be allowed more that it is at the moment." (Bishop)

Finally, in view of the importance of the significance of belief in common amongst Catholics who participate in the Eucharist, it is worth juxtaposing two views, one from a non-parochial priest, and one from a respondent no longer in official ministry.

"I'm not sure all Catholics should receive. They are no longer quiet before mass. Some do not understand the Blessed Sacrament."

"What's the problem? If you go into any Catholic Church on Sunday morning and ask the adults to tell you what they understand as the real presence of Christ, every answer will be different. We are living under the myth that there is a body of truth which we all accept at the same time... If any Christian feels they can participate in the Eucharist it means they have taken serious decisions about who they are."

Women priests

As is well known, the Roman Catholic Church does not allow the ordination of women to the priesthood. Further, the present Pope has reiterated that the subject is closed for discussion. For this reason, interviewers were very careful to respect any indication on the part of respondents that they did not wish to discuss the subject. As will be seen from the verbatim comments below, talking about the subject was not a problem. Indeed, some respondents were more concerned about the prohibition on open debate than they were about the issue itself.

One parish priest claimed not to know that there was any problem:

"I didn't even know that. It's irrelevant. We all know it won't happen in his [the present Pope's] lifetime, and it may not happen in the next one's lifetime either, but it will come."

(Parish priest)

the prohibition on open debate

In this research 19 of the 65 respondents were actively **in favour** of the ordination of women to the priesthood. It should be said immediately that 14 of these were priests who had resigned their active ministry.

Perhaps more surprisingly, the research showed that only 20 of the 65 were actively **opposed** to the ordination of women. The other respondents declared themselves willing to accept the Church's teaching at present, but said that they themselves were either agnostic on the subject, or had no objection to the idea of women priests, and many went further, saying they expected this to happen (if not in the current Pope's lifetime).

The positions of opposition to women priests, of support for their ministry and acceptance of current Church teaching will now be discussed.

Those opposed

Three kinds of opposition can be discerned. The first looks to the example of Christ.

> *"It's a sign that the priest is Christ to the congregation. Christ was not a woman. That icon means that priesthood is male. Certain women would feel that they would want to be called, but they aren't."* (Seminarian)

> *"The greatest sexist is God himself. He created them male and female with different qualities and attributes. The priest is acting in the person of Christ who became man, and not a woman. Therefore, the Church is quite right."* (Non-parochial)

> *"Women priests are an impossibility because Christ ordained none. In addition, scripturally Christ is the groom of the Church."* (Recently ordained)

Secondly, opposition to women priests can be derived from ideas of tradition. It can be accepted that it is a difficult issue, and that nothing in the female personality makes women less spiritual than the male, but

> *"Historically Christ's time was a unique time that sealed the way things were done... If we had no men, then we would move to women priests."* (Parish priest)

the example of Christ

ideas of tradition

> "It has been the doctrine of the Church from the earliest times. It has only been questioned in the modern age, and the answer has been definitely given as far as I am concerned." (Parish priest)

> "If we believe that Jesus set up a Church, he gave apostles to that Church, and their tradition from an early point on points in a certain direction. To deny this is either to say Jesus is wrong or He's not in the Church anymore, and we begin to lose everything else then. It's because the priesthood is not just another ministry; it's the whole supernatural realm. Priesthood is not a right." (Seminarian)

The third strand of argument against the ordination of women takes the form of a strong defence of the Church's teaching. So, closure of discussion is seen as steering the discussion away from pointless debate and preventing heated and therefore unhelpful controversy.

> "Concerning women's ordination I would have to say that is the teaching of the Church and it is pointless to discuss it endlessly on the assumption that the Church would change. Of its nature a discussion would be pointless." (Recently ordained)

> "It does not seem to be God's will at the moment… It would upset things after 2,000 years of tradition." (Recently ordained)

anxieties about a threat to unity

Some respondents, looking at the recent experience of the Anglican Church, express anxieties about a threat to unity if the Roman Catholic Church's position were to be reversed.

> "There is no theological reason [against the ordination of women], but on-going tradition means it would be a big step. I approve of the Church's caution. There are several difficulties that need to be worked through slowly: the Anglicans are now a divided Church." (Seminarian)

The rule against women priests "cannot be justified theologically but do we want the Catholic Church to turn into a Church like the Anglican…? Questions of the unity of the Church ring alarm bells for me. I would be happy to accept women priests if the Church said 'yes' but the issue we should be looking at is celibacy and married priests." (Seminarian)

Those supporting the ordination of women
Support for women priests can take the form of denying that the appeal to tradition simply trumps any other move, or it can question the force of arguments from the action of Jesus:

> "I have no problem with that. There's no reason why not. Just because we haven't had them, it doesn't mean we can't have them." (Parish priest)

> "I'm in favour of the ordination of women. The Pope says, you know, Jesus didn't do it, therefore we may not do it. That principle is false. You can say that about religious orders. Jesus didn't start a religious order, so St. Benedict is not allowed to either." (Resigned)

> "I'm totally fed up with Catholic press arguments that women cannot be priests because Christ did not ordain his mother. It's theological clap-trap. Jesus did not ordain anybody." (Resigned)

Those whose experience has involved working with women priests give more weight than those opposed to women's ordination to the special gifts women bring.

> "I work with women priests of other denominations. I have difficulty accepting the Church's position. Nothing I've read has hit me as to why we can't do it. Women can bring things to situations that men can't. We complement each other... The whole idea of not allowing discussion is not a viable decision to take. It's an abuse of authority, not a use of it." (Non-parochial)

Those accepting the Church's position
Some seem to hold out for the possibility of change but over a very long period of time.

> "I suspect that the Holy Spirit should be given the opportunity to help us... I know that the anthropology of 2000 years ago had men always being in positions of leadership, but I would not at the moment say yes... I think that the Holy Spirit has to give us a lot of insights and development yet." (Bishop)

> "Emotionally I've got no problem with it. Culturally, yes. Theologically, I can see the theological argument against it, but

Women can bring things to situations that men can't

> *I'm not all persuaded by it... maybe in 50 years we can look at it again..."* (Bishop)

call for theological discussion

Others appear to find the present state of the Church's mind on this issue unclear, and call for theological discussion of what is an entirely new question which cannot be adequately addressed by a simple appeal to a tradition which evolved in a different socio-political context.

> *"I stick with the Church's teaching at the moment... Attitudes may change... Why can't they have an open forum, or debate? Get the best theologians to look at the ontological significance, at tradition, research it over a few years, and do a report..."*
> (Recently ordained)

One non-parochial priest, accepting that the issue depends entirely on papal decision in the future, commented wryly that "meanwhile we should do all we can to change his mind". However, some of those accepting present decisions seem to do so on the basis of a prognosis of the likely chances of effecting any change. For them it is a battle that cannot be won.

This position can be taken even in the face of the positive experience of the work of women priests:

> *"Having worked with an Anglican woman priest at the hospice, I feel she brought a warmth to the ministry which I appreciated. At present the Catholic Church feels it isn't possible, and from the way the Pope has spoken that it would never be possible. Personally I'm agnostic about it. If the Church felt it would be a good idea, I'd happily go along with it, but it's not something I'd fight for."* (Recently ordained)

Contraception

The card shown to respondents contained the word "contraception", which was intended to be shorthand for the whole of this controversial debate. However, many respondents were quick to point out that the card should have said "artificial birth control". They explained that "natural" birth control is permitted by the Church, though one bishop considered that the Church had failed people by not developing natural family planning scientifically.

In our non-generalisable sample only a small number of respondents (14 of 65) gave unequivocal support to Humanae Vitae. Around a third of all respondents had difficulty with the teaching of Humanae Vitae, and believed that the Church should change its current stance on this issue. The remaining respondents gave what could be considered a pragmatic view. They saw Humanae Vitae as the ideal, but for pastoral reasons did not stress its message within their own constituencies.

Very few respondents believed that birth control in itself was wrong (and some explained the principles – and claimed success rates – of natural family planning to the interviewer). The *method* of family planning however was all important to some respondents. For these very reasons, some respondents found it difficult to argue that all acts of human intercourse should be open to the possibility of new life.

The vast majority of those who have resigned their active ministries were opposed to the Church's current teaching on birth control, but on this issue the majority of both seminarians and the recently ordained (who have been fairly *"orthodox"* in their views about the issues discussed so far) also had some doubts about current teaching.

Those agreeing with Humanae Vitae

This relatively small group of respondents, often spoke with great depth of feeling on this issue. This can derive from viewing Humanae Vitae as an attempt to warn society against the evils consequent on contraception.

> *"Contraception has succeeded in destroying families and destroying the concept of the true nature of sexuality. I'm in full agreement with Pope Paul VI's Humanae Vitae… If you go back to presenting a reasoned faith in accordance with nature, contraception contradicts that image, procreation is all about life, contraception and abortion are all about death."* (Recently ordained)

> *"Humanae Vitae said that once the contraceptive mentality is adopted, child abuse, abortion, the abuse of women would increase. Abortion is just the ultimate form of contraception.*

few respondents believed that birth control in itself was wrong

a social warning

> *Human life is degraded and devalued by the prevalent use of contraception."* (Recently ordained)
>
> *"Contraception destroys any concept of the true nature of sexuality. It is all about death."* (Recently ordained)
>
> *"I'm wholeheartedly with the Church on this one, not just from a level of principle, but from past experience of health problems and all sorts of other things arising from the current use of contraception."* (Non-parochial)

A variant of this theme is to raise the level of the teaching of Humanae Vitae to the level of the prophetic.

> *"I'm in full agreement with the teaching given in 1968 in Humanae Vitae, which I think is a very prophetic statement of the Church, not easy to accept, but the Christian life isn't easy either."* (Parish priest)
>
> *"I think it was quite a prophetic document... I think it's a very difficult question, and again, I would never take the view that Catholic women should just produce babies on the trot. I take the general teaching of the Church, about responsible parenthood... in the past, they abstained at appropriate times, and so on. Which again, is totally counter-cultural..."* (Bishop)

any problems were surmountable

A Seminarian considered that any problems were surmountable through the power of the Holy Spirit, at the same time as he looked to an earlier age:

> *"It's a very difficult issue. You have to come down to love and listening to what people's problems are. God does not give us any burden that we cannot carry. Unnatural contraception can interfere with total union and total love and with life... It is a hard teaching but one of the Holy Spirit, and we are celibate with the Holy Spirit's power and not on our own. You can practice natural family planning with the Holy Spirit's help. When people had a lot of children there was love and simplicity."*

Finally, any difficulties with the universal reception of the teaching of Paul VI are located not in its reasoning but in failures of those who find the teaching difficult for socio-cultural or intellectual reasons.

> "I agree with the doctrine as enunciated by Pope Paul VI in Humanae Vitae. I always have done. It is disputed and I understand the reasons. But I consider it wholly right although it is difficult in the present age. It's extremely difficult for it to be accepted and convincingly preached, but I don't think the Church can change its position." (Parish priest)

> "The problem with contraception is that people want to have pleasure without responsibility... Very often we are telling people things they don't have the ability to understand, they aren't well instructed." (Non-parochial)

The notion of reasons that might be considered selfish can be contrasted to reasons that are unselfish. As one bishop remarked: "I think we haven't heard the last of it... if birth control by whatever means is done for selfish reasons, it's bad. If it is done for truly loving reasons, the method doesn't matter."

Those who have difficulty with Humanae Vitae

Many different kinds of difficulty arise in relation to official teaching on artificial contraception. First, its controversial nature. So, one non-parochial priest said:

> "I don't bring up the question very much because it's so controversial... I don't go around shouting about it, I wouldn't preach about it because it's very personal. I **would** preach on chastity. There is now qualified opposition to Papal teaching, and some support."

And a bishop expressed profound unease at the way in which papal teaching was being ignored:

> "And yet here is an official and fairly solemn teaching being ignored by many in the Church, and that causes me a lot of anxiety that papal teaching has not been received by the Church."

At the opposite end of the spectrum of opinion are those who cannot believe that Humanae Vitae should have been papal teaching in the first place.

> "The current teaching should have ended with Paul VI,

its controversial nature

because the majority of theologians thought that the whole idea against contraception was based in a false philosophical premise and therefore was wrong." (Resigned)

"Pope Paul VI made a bad mistake, and I say it with all possible respect, and in the 30 years since then there's been no convincing theological argument to uphold the Pope's case. The whole thing is run on terror. Priests know they will not be ordained if they don't subscribe to it, and bishops know that a man won't be appointed a bishop unless he gives public support. I'm afraid to say that the whole thing is one great big deception based upon fear." (Resigned)

teaching to be applied within marriage

No one from any of the other groupings took a similar view. Rather those who had some difficulty with Humanae Vitae sought to renegotiate, as it were, the terms of the teaching. So, for some the greatest area of difficulty was that the teaching was to be applied *within* marriage, as well as outside it. One recently ordained priest said he would use condoms if he were married.

"In marriage relationships, there ought to be more scope for artificial means of contraception, if that is based on a mature decision in conjunction with spiritual advisers. Premarital sex equals pleasure without commitment. There are a lot of deep spiritual reasons why the Church teaches what it does on contraception – something about a complete openness which some form of contraception deny. The teaching is for committed Christians." (Seminarian)

"As an Anglican, my wife and I were allowed to practise contraception within marriage. As Catholics, we are not. So we follow the teaching of the Church. I'm not going to say the teaching of the Church is wrong, I don't think it is, but I think it is rather too prescriptive. Say you have half a dozen children and you are capable of having more – is it the wisest thing in the world to have more? I think we could conduct the argument more along Anglican lines, but only for those who are married – chastity applies to everyone." (Recently ordained)

"I don't see any problem with contraception, I really don't in the least. And when people come to me in the confessional, I just remind them that a sin is only a sin when you know it to

> be a sin, and if you are actually doing something that in the depths of your conscience you know to be right for you and for the life you are living with your husband, that is not a sin. Promiscuity is a sin, but to use some means of contraception within the loving relationship of a marriage is a different issue." (Recently ordained)

A pragmatic view

Those accepting current teaching tend to stress the place of individual decision, of conscience, and of individual circumstances. "Contraception", said one parish priest, *"does not create a great pastoral problem at the moment. Virtually all practice it. An attitude of mind that is contraceptive is not a good Christian attitude; it's a selfish attitude – we'll have the second child after the second car. It's also wrong (for a married couple) to live as brother and sister or to have as many children as God will send. You have to leave adult Christians to make up their own mind."*

individual decision

> "I feel unqualified to speak about it. Facing facts, most people have made up their own minds and they don't come seeking advice. I would find it very difficult to answer them. I would try to get them to use their own conscience." (Parish priest)

> "I see the Church's teaching as giving the ideal, trying to preserve the human within sexuality… having said that I know that many Catholics find this hard to understand and so they do what they can. And pastors… try not to force a teaching which might be too hard for people at certain times in their lives." (Bishop)

The validity of Anglican Orders

In 1896, Pope Leo XIII issued a decree, which declared that Anglican Orders were *"absolutely null and utterly void"*. The somewhat hysterical tone of that judgement, based on an interpretation of the state of historical research and also of concern that recognition would lead to an exodus from the then current Roman Church has not always been tempered in more recent times.

Those who give unquestioning support to present teaching emphasise the sacrificial nature of the Roman Catholic Eucharist, and unbroken though undeveloped tradition.

121

Mass as sacrifice

"A priest is someone who offers sacrifice. In the 500 years of Anglican history, 99.9% of Anglican ministers have not thought they were offering any sacrifice." (Parish priest)

"The Anglicans denied the idea of the sacrifice of the Mass, and to us that was essential. People say it would be nice if we recognised the validity of Anglican orders, but if you read the Book of Common Prayer and the 39 Articles there is no way you can accept this." (Non-parochial)

"They can only have valid orders if they are ordained by a bishop who has lineage with the Apostles. If the Eucharist is seen as anything less than the sacrifice, if it's just the meal, then it isn't priesthood and it's not the Catholic faith. It can cause major division, but if you want everyone to come to the truth you've got to tell it as it is." (Seminarian)

"We have our own traditions. If you want to be part of that, join the Catholic Church." (Non-parochial)

"No, I don't think [Anglican Orders[are valid. They have cut away from the Church so we wouldn't be true to ourselves or them." (Parish priest)

"The sincerity and belief are there, but it doesn't make it reality. You might have a polished crystal which you believe is a diamond, and you treasure it and pass it on for generations, but it doesn't make it a diamond." (Recently ordained)

the historical basis

Those less sure of the Church's position reflect on their own experience or doubt the historical basis of Apostolical Curae.

"What changed my perception was working with an Anglican hospital chaplain on pastoral placement. I shared everything with him and saw how effective he was. Not much divided us, but he wasn't ordained by a valid bishop… I do not rubbish the Christian witness of other ministries." (Recently ordained)

"I think we should have another look at that. I'm not saying that they are valid, but in the light of modern historical research, I think that the 1896 document should be reassessed." (Bishop)

> "The declaration of 1896 that they're invalid seems to be lunatic. I don't think you can describe the Archbishop of Canterbury as a layman. The whole thing is nonsense, so arcane and far-fetched as to be irrelevant. They are valid in the sense that they are working as recognised priests and leaders in their churches." (Resigned)

Sacramental participation of the divorced

Once again some respondents correctly took issue with the shorthand used to describe this subject, and pointed out that the wording should have read *"admittance to Communion of the divorced and remarried"*.

For virtually all respondents, this was one of the most difficult issues to discuss. Very few could talk about teaching that refuses Communion to those who have divorced and remarried without reference to the pain and distress the ruling has caused to their own parishioners and even, as will be seen, to members of their own family.

The biggest stumbling block was the idea that remarriage had somehow become the *"worst"* of all sins, worse than rape or murder. Most respondents were unhappy with the idea that should an individual make a mistake in their choice of marriage partner, or – worse – should that partner ill treat or beat them, if they divorced and later remarried they would then be excluded from sharing communion for the rest of their life. One respondent gave the dramatic example of a prison warder who had been divorced and remarried having to escort a child murderer to Mass. The child murderer was allowed to receive communion, the remarried person was not.

remarriage the "worst of all sins"

The following extracts, from two recently ordained priests, perhaps sum up the arguments on each side:

> "If you flout the rules of the Church, how can you expect a full role in the Church? Whilst I recognise the extreme pain they suffer, if you are not fully behind what the Church teaches, if you decide to do something other than the Church teaches, then you have to accept the consequences as hard as they may be."

123

> "I think we've got it wrong. It's about inclusiveness, forgiveness. The Church's attitude causes so much pain. My mum divorced because of a violent marriage, and married my Catholic dad. He is effectively excommunicated because he is technically living in sin, and my mum can't become a Catholic because she is a divorcee and hasn't enough witnesses to have her marriage annulled... I think it's scandalous that you can be a rapist, paedophile or murderer, be reconciled to the Church and receive the sacraments, but if you've made a mistake, or been in a violent marriage, or someone committed adultery, you are punished for the rest of your life, cut off from the sacramental life of the Church. The sacraments are there for healing. They need healing above all. The Church needs to change."

This section of the interview provided a classic example of respondents being torn between their personal feelings and the teachings of the Church. In the event, around half of respondents wanted to see Church teaching on this issue re-considered. This drops to two fifths if those who have resigned their active ministry are excluded. However, even those respondents who claimed to support Church teaching went on to express their own deep pain at the situation.

Those who support current Church's teaching

Those who supported the Church's teaching on this issue went on to advance arguments why the teaching should remain as it is. However, even these respondents expressed their own deep pain at the situation.

> "I agree with the teaching on that. It is so explicit in the Gospels. I know a lot of divorced people who are re-married, and I would do anything to relieve their anxiety... that is the sacrifice that you have to make for the sacredness and indissolubility of marriage." (Parish priest)

> "It's very difficult – there are a number of people in this parish, and my last parish. It's a very sad and painful situation for them, and for me as well. But I cannot see what one can do. To do otherwise is to accept marriage after divorce as a true marriage, and one cannot do that. I know lots of people, some of whom I consider my friends, in this situation. It has caused

me considerable pain and worry, but I see the point of if."

(Parish priest)

"It is one of the biggest problems. I don't know how it will be resolved. It's not the divorce, it's remarriage. I want to help them, yet I want to keep the law of the Church. I have tremendous sadness for people in that situation." (Parish priest)

"It's a difficult one. My nephew is divorced and receiving the Holy Sacrament. Divorce is not a sin. A divorced person can receive the sacraments. It is only when they re-marry that they can't. I agree with that." (Non-parochial)

"The Church has certain principles. It's impossible, and very sad. But that's just the way it is." (Seminarian)

"I would hold to the Church's teaching… but I do feel hugely sorry for the people in that situation." (Seminarian)

"They are in a position which objectively contradicts the teaching of Christ, and I would uphold the Church's position. Unless that changes, they can't receive the sacraments."

(Recently ordained)

One or two respondents were concerned about the way the Church handles annulments, awarding them to some and refusing them to others. And a few felt that annulments were the equivalent of divorce by the back door, and a way of getting round the problem rather than facing up to it.

"Either people are divorced and can't get married again, or they can. We can't go on the way we are doing, dishing out annulments, getting round it like they do in America. We either have a doctrine or we don't: it's deception otherwise. We're doing justice to some people and not to others." (Non-parochial)

Those who would like to see this issue reconsidered

The majority of participants in this study argued for a change in Church teaching. Many of them are already in the position of going against that teaching because they cannot turn people away from Communion.

they cannot turn people away

125

"Good people don't receive the sacraments: people receive the sacraments. They are not given as a reward for being good, they are given as a means... I'm not defending divorce... but on a practical level, if someone came to me and said they really wanted Holy Communion... I have never refused the sacrament in over 30 years to anybody but drunks." (Parish priest)

"I think it's vital in the future that people are allowed to take part... the reality of it is in our world so many marriages aren't permanent anymore. I think it is punishment enough, the breakdown of marriage, but to deprive them of the sacrament I don't think is justified." (Non-parochial)

"With divorce in my family background, I don't think Christ should be denied to anybody. Whatever the Church says, when it comes to the crunch, would Christ want to be denied to anybody?" (Seminarian)

"It's difficult... to deprive someone of that central part of their faith is a real kick in the teeth when they need the support of their faith and what the sacrament can bring." (Seminarian)

"The Church has just been horrible to these people, punishing them almost... I'd like to see a change in this... people have been hurt enough: they want Jesus and the Eucharist and they can't have them." (Recently ordained)

"We should always try to do the right thing lovingly, and say to anybody who came privately and wasn't going to make a big issue out of it, yes, go to communion." (Recently ordained)

"I think Jesus was about giving people new beginnings and fresh starts. And there are many, many people who are the innocent parties in divorce who have been prevented now from either receiving the Eucharist or having an intimate loving relationship with someone in the future. And I think that can't equate with the Christ who says 'Come to me all you who are heavy-laden, and I will give you rest...' ." (Resigned)

"I disagree with the Church wholeheartedly here. Jesus said the sick need the doctor, not the healthy... the Church decided to deprive people of the help they need, the Eucharist. The Church kicks them when they are down." (Resigned)

"I think there has to be some special pastoral care for the divorced, because people don't get divorced for fun. It's a big trauma in someone's life." (Resigned)

"Some way round this problem has to be found." (Parish priest)

It is not surprising that the Bishops too had concerns about this issue suggesting solutions in the form of faster annulments:

"It's a big problem, because could more people not have their first marriages declared null and void, because in many cases they were not really marriages at all...?" (Bishop)

"I'd like to see our marriage tribunals more effective... I think it's terrible the way we keep people hanging about." (Bishop)

"This is a very agonising situation, and I don't think we have heard the last of it... we certainly have to preserve the sanctity of marriage, but I don't think we have the fullest understanding of what constitutes a marriage... if a marriage has long since ceased to exist, and the children have been cared for in every sense, it seems to me to be such past history that only theoretically are these people married..." (Bishop)

Conclusion

The above findings may be considered surprising by some. The Roman Catholic Church is popularly represented as an organisation which is traditional, conservative, and very much of a single mind. This research suggests that this is not the case. Even taking out of the equation the views of those priests who have resigned the active ministry, the results suggest that there are many points of view among priests in the Catholic Church, not all of them coinciding with current Church teaching.

At this point we would repeat the caveat about using numbers in qualitative research. However, given the subject of the research, we are aware that some will find it useful to see a table of the findings. Thus, Table 3 below summarises the percentages *in favour of a change to, or reconsideration of,* current Church teaching. The first figure shows percentages in favour when those who have resigned their active ministry are **excluded** (i.e. 50 respondents); the second figure shows the position for **all** respondents (i.e. 65 respondents).

"Some way round this problem has to be found."

These figures, of course, do not show all the different shades and levels of conviction about each subject: the earlier, more detailed, analysis provides the fuller picture.

TABLE FIVE

A summary of views – those looking for change

Issue	50 resp. (excludes resigned) %	65 resp. (all resp.) %
Marriage should be an option for priests	68	75
Celibacy should not be compulsory for priests	56	66
The admittance of the divorced and re-married to communion should be re-considered	42	54
Communion should be offered to Christians of other denominations	26	42
The validity of Anglican Orders should be re-considered	22	34
Artificial birth control should be re-considered	12	31
Women should be able to become Roman Catholic priests	10	29

This table summarises the views of respondents within the sample. It cannot be taken as applying to the generality of the clergy.

Chapter Seven

GENERAL CONCLUSION

IT MAY BE THE CASE THAT *"Authority in the Church is more than a socio-political reality"*, as the chairman of the American Bishops' Committee on Priestly Formation stated. However, his definition of the source for an improved formation, suggests precisely the primacy of an historical understanding of a developing socio-political reality. *"A proper understanding is discerned only from the de facto tradition of theological teaching rooted in the apostolic era and developed through the centuries."* (Hermrick and Hoge, 1991, p.45) More significantly, we should at least attempt an understanding of authority in the Church by exploring the extent to which socio-political reality casts light on current concerns.

A number of concepts of a socio-political nature are available: pre-Vatican II/post Vatican II; left-right; traditional/liberal. The range of views presented in the foregoing chapters suggests that more than a simple dichotomy is required. Moreover, the substance of the interviews indicates the instability of these terms. One recently ordained man said: *"I would like to be considered right-wing because this would mean the Church had changed toward the left."* Another said that in a South American situation he would be in support of the poor, because he could not stand suffering. Another priest referred explicitly to Vatican II in connection with a question on changes in formation and the role of the laity, but placed a particular gloss on both. In relation to the former he said: *"I would seek to implement Vatican II on formation, involving a year on spirituality, the idea of mortification and of rectifying camp, clerical dress, Latin, and a non critical attitude to the teaching of the magisterium."* (Recently ordained)

A respondent pointed to the situational character of a distinction between conservative and liberal. *"I'm not a loyal dissenter, I'm completely mainstream Catholic in the line of Vatican II. Because of the peculiar situation of conservative backlash it looks as if I am a rebel…"*

The distinction between left and right orientations is a commonplace in political analysis, but the meaning of such

more than a simple dichotomy

difference in points on a scale is by no means clear. In relation to priests the recent American survey concluded that the distinction did not advance our understanding of contemporary priesthood.

The discussion in the previous chapters has frequently pointed to distinctions that go beyond the purely dichotomous. We should also emphasise that the aim of any characterisation is not the identification of distinct groups of people holding the same coherent set of beliefs and attitudes, but the discernment of tendencies or orientation available from the experience of the priests and seminarians studied. If these can be identified they should help to meet what the American study concluded to be *"the need for a compelling theology of priesthood for the years ahead. Due to rising expectations of priests by laity; broadening of ministries, expanding lay staffs in parishes, and manifold innovations in Church life, priests face confusion about their central identity…"*

The research material presented suggests that a combination of judgements on the role and status of the priest, and a view of the Church as closed, organisational, or communitarian produces discernible different orientations towards the questions and topics we have examined. Priesthood can be viewed as sacred, as functional, and as communitarian. The Church can be seen as closed, as primarily an organisation or a developing mission. To illustrate the three orientations we re-visit in the main the words respondents used in answer to particular questions.

Sacred priest – closed Church

Sacred priest

A sacred view of the person of the priest can be seen either in a kind of identification of the priest with Christ – as one priest phrased it – *"being a pygmy in giant's clothing"* or in a sense that the priest acts as a direct conduit of God or salvation to the people. *"For me that is what priesthood is about, giving my life to God and hopefully to bring God to those around you."* (Seminarian) A newly ordained priest believed that priesthood constituted *"an identification with Christ, standing in the place of Christ, doing the things Christ did… admiring other priests as a young boy gave me the idea this was a very sacred office"*. A non-parochial priest spoke of the *"priest representing Christ to the community… We represent Christ at the altar."*

a direct conduit of God

Here a priest re-presents Christ, and he does this primarily as a member of a sacramental and sacrificial priesthood. This salvific function can take one of two forms. In the first the Church is, as it were, abstracted from a personal relationship with God and becomes *"almost a tool"* or as another priest put it, scaffolding. In the second the sacramental plays an essential role in the integration of celebration and creation of the community, though some would see the sacrament almost exclusively in terms of the Eucharist. *"The ministry is based on the Eucharist. The Eucharist is at the centre of the life of the Church. The significance of the priesthood is as profound as the Eucharist. Priest, Eucharist, and community are not separate entities."* (Seminarian) Priests with a sacral orientation sometimes use a phrase more common in a communitarian approach, being with the people, but this refers to a sacramental mode – being with people and administering the sacraments at times of life events, such as marriage and birth. *"You can be with people, celebrating at the low points and high points."* (Non-parochial)

Views that *"priesthood has to do with a man's identity as a person"* (Recently ordained) and that it is *"of the essence of the Church… The Church is not simply a gathering of like-minded people with a person charged with certain functions."* (Recently ordained) accompany a strong belief in the changes effected by ordination. *"We are told in the Church's teaching we are ontologically changed. I believe we are somehow marked, consecrated. You don't suddenly after ordination find it harder to lose your temper, easier to pray, but at a fundamental level it is different. I've certainly noticed when I've gone into situations where I don't know what to do, there's an inner force, an inner strength."* (Recently ordained). A parish priest responded: *"We are certainly taught it changes you. An indelible mark on your soul. It is not a question just of doing certain tasks; the hand of God is at work. He gives you the grace. You do walk with God, and we have His guidance."* Another parish priest spoke of ontological change and believed that even if the priest no longer celebrated the sacraments he would still remain a man apart. A non-parochial priest spoke, as did several respondents of the grace given at ordination: *"You are given grace to be in a new and different relationship with Christ… At the consecration – 'This is my body' – he speaks in the person of Christ. In some sense he does this in the rest of the service; in some sense everybody does when they speak the truth."*

ontologically changed

The implicit questions in a notion that everybody, and not just the ordained, can speak in the person rather that the name of Christ are not explored in an orientation that emphasises the sacerdotal as sacred. The distinction between priests and lay people is essential and not a matter of difference in job description. The priest is seen as set apart, as Christ in this perspective was set apart from his apostles. The priesthood is a unique way of sharing in the ministerial priesthood of Christ.

authority as sacred

Such a view has consequences, of course, for issues of authority and governance. A recently ordained priest described his authority as sacred:

> *"The authority I have is a sacred authority essentially. For example, I could theoretically refuse absolution. I don't often think about it. What you do as a priest you do with authority when you are doing sacred things, because it's God's action through you and it's done with the backing of the whole Church. There is an awful authority behind or through what we do. Perhaps it's a good thing we don't consider it too much."*

Others stress that the priest governs in the place of Christ or that bishops alone can govern the Church. There is recognition of the wisdom of using lay expertise, but lay people have no right to be consulted.

> *"Whilst priests and bishops would be wise to make use of lay expertise it also behoves the laity to make an act of faith, and say the Church is God's Church and He has chosen to manage the Church through His ordained ministers."* (Recently ordained)

"We might as well be Quakers"

A belief in this ordering is not compatible with the idea that lay people are the Church and what should be questioned is the role of the ordained minister. This is dismissed as more applicable to other religious groups – *"We might as well be Quakers"* (Parish priest); *"We do not have a Presbyterian model. Ours has community from the people of God and also an ordained ministry from God Himself. We teach what the apostles taught and are ordained to back that. Special grace is given to the ordained minister which has to do with the mystery of the Church itself."* (Parish priest)

CHAPTER SEVEN: GENERAL CONCLUSION

This grace can be brought to bear on the problems facing the Church, and those thinking of priesthood as sacred and the Church as closed see these in characteristically *"churchy"* terms. A recently ordained priest believed that the main challenge *"revolves around authority because authority is being challenged, and the fruit of that challenge is not a good fruit if it brings disharmony."* Others point to a lack of faith:

> *"A lack of faith amongst people. People don't understand about the Church. In an American survey 67% of Catholics did not believe in the Blessed Sacrament. The only part of the Church which is flourishing are the traditionalists... Flourishing because it comes back to the mass. They are very clear what they believe, and have a very strict regime in their seminaries. Orders that are very modern seem to be dying out... The bishop won't discuss the flourishing of traditional orders. Authority does not want to be disturbed. The moral teaching of the Church is weak at the moment. You cannot live together and be good Catholics. I expect people to sin, but not to say I'm right because I'm doing it."* (Non-parochial)

Another priest pointed to special difficulties in relation to rapid changes in the liturgy and the arrangements in Church buildings:

> *"People cannot identify the Church now as it was when they were younger. It's such a big leap and we've lost a lot of people."* (Parish priest)

It is as if pervasive notions of growth in personal faith, and a faith journey which presumably can be measured in terms of approximation to a goal cannot be applied to the Church.

Dimensions of a closed Church

The Church can be described as relatively closed along at least three dimension: decision-making, membership and teaching. First, lay people are excluded from such key decisions as the appointment of priests and bishops. The possibility may be admitted, but, in the words of a recently ordained priest:

> *"The drawback is that Christ called and sent out. Christ's call is articulated by the bishop who knows the priests and parishes. The Church can create so many committees."*

lay people are excluded

133

Another warned of the danger of politics:

> "... you get the kind of bishop the priests want, not what God wants. It is sometimes good for us not to have the priest we want. We should have more faith in the Church."

Others drew a parallel with other professions: lay people should have no more part in the selection of priests than they have in the choice of candidates for accountancy.

Second, a closed Church implies a keen appreciation of the boundaries of membership and the virtues of loyalty.

> "To dissent from Church teaching is to go off on your own tangent. You can dissent over taste and politics but if we believe in one truth to dissent from the truth is to say we are calling God a liar." (Seminarian)

> "If you join a club or political party you are expected to espouse their policies. One can question in order to seek understanding. There is no place at all for protest. There is a deposit of faith" (Recently ordained)

> "Once you are part of an organisation you must be loyal, and if you are not loyal you should leave" (Parish priest)

Third, the Church can be described as closed in so far as changes in practices are ruled out by unchangeable teaching. So, those Catholics who divorce and re-marry cannot receive communion.

unchangeable teaching

> "Marriage is a public act and to get divorced and re-marry invalidly is to say in a public way I am not accepting the Church's teaching." (Non-parochial)

> "I won't give communion to other Christians, so I won't to divorced people. I want to sustain the idea of sacramental marriage. We either have a doctrine or we don't. Otherwise it's deception." (Non-parochial)

> "The Church **cannot** change the ideal of life-long marriage."
> (Recently ordained)

Similarly, in relation to the ordination of women it is argued, as we have seen, that:

> *"Historically Christ's time was a unique time that sealed the way things were done. The Church would never use any other symbol than water because Christ used it. If we had no men, then we would move to women priests."* (Parish priest)

> *"There could not be women priests. Jesus never made any, never ordained them. It must be men."* (Parish priest)

Priests as functionaries in an organisational Church

In contrast to the 'sealed' time of Christ as putting an absolute limit on change, it is possible to see priesthood as a historical development, just like ecclesial development.

> *"The Church invented priesthood: somebody had to be president of the growing Christian community. It could have been different. If I want to see how priesthood has changed I look at the papacy and how that has changed. For example, there was a martial papacy."* (Parish priest)

In this perspective the reasons for seeking holy orders may shift – from what is God's will or the idea that a priest could be almost born with a vocation – towards an emphasis on what the Church decides in the individual case. It may also lead to a particular prioritising of the various ministries of a priest:

> *"The role of the priest is to exercise a pastoral ministry, to act on behalf of the official church as a person who shares the bishops responsibility for other people in the community in which you find yourself. On the religious side it is to live out a life based on the scriptures and to share that practically with other people. Preaching is calling people to the Gospel. The sacraments are also crucial."* (Seminarian)

If priesthood is, in the words of a respondent, the servant of the Church, a more positive approach to the functional aspects of the priestly ministry seems to give second place to the belief that:

> *"We have to make great efforts that it [the priesthood] does not slide into a functional role through prayer and meeting people."*
> (Parish priest)

priesthood as a historical development

servant of the Church

This in turn gives way to a conviction that: *"letting the buck stop with the priest is the service he gives the community."* (Parish priest)

Another parish priest suggested that:

> *"In the main part if [the priesthood] is functional; there's a lot of administration. Most of the time I am a functional priest. You never know who will be on the 'phone or calling at the door, and there are certain set things like services, but you have to be there for people and people's problems which are very different. Dealing with the school that brings all sorts of problems which you can never forecast."*

promises made to the institution

Whilst this orientation does not exclude use of the term ontological to describe any change effected by ordination, the interpretation of change relies less on a mark on the soul or a change at the level of being and more on the implications of promises made to the institution or the results of long-term behavioural change.

> *"There is an ontological change... in as much as a person makes a solemn promise to God to take a particular role in the Church."* (Seminarian)

> *"I suppose I have changed. Your attitudes change because of the promises at ordination – obedience and celibacy."* (Parish priest)

> *"The priesthood is supposed to change you. Of necessity, if people come to you for advice about spiritual things, you have to have some knowledge, that's why we do two years philosophy and three years theology. It's no good me being a priest if I don't have something spiritual in my life. You have in confession to show the rationality of faith and that type of thing. Once you deal with people's problems that will change you. It makes you more broadminded. The sufferings of people are quite extreme at times. Even saying mass properly will change you."* (Non-parochial)

A belief that *"we are getting back to the priesthood of all believers, like One Body but all different parts"* (Seminarian), poses two problems for the organisation. First, how are the parts ordered? As we have seen, one possibility is to see the ministerial priesthood as a unique ministry, as an essential part of the mystery of the Church. However, an organisational conception of the Church stresses difference in contribution rather than any superiority.

> *"You cannot say you are holier. There is a different job to be done, as nursing is different from banking. In the past the differences would be in terms of higher and better."* (Parish priest)

In reply to the question on the distinction between holy orders and the common priesthood of the baptised another parish priest said: *"To answer yes suggests we are raised above the priesthood of the faithful. This would not be the mind of the Church. Not higher but different in nature and form."* Yet reference to the two ministries as simply different overlooks the ways in which the role of the priest attracts very special regard from parishioners or the high expectations a priest may entertain of his own behaviour.

special regard from parishioners

> *"Parishioners bleed when the priest leaves. People treat you with deference, not for personal qualities but because you are a priest. It's the "father" they love not the person. Orders bestow the love of the people on you. They will love you come what may, and that changes you because we are in a most privileged position."* (Parish priest)

The constraints of the role of priest are described by a recently ordained respondent:

> *"People are always conscious of your being a priest. One has to be more circumspect in the things one does and the things one says. When holding together that community you can't always be what you want… Within the community one must be aware of exercising too much power. You are given an immense amount of power and I am amazed at the respect people have for the priesthood, for all priests, for the role, so you mustn't get big-headed about it."*

The second problem with the notion of an equality between priestly and lay ministry arises from the issue of legitimacy: how is the extensive part now played by priests in the governance of the Church – at least as seen my many respondents – justified?

the issue of legitimacy

137

Collaboration between priests and people is a favoured and persuasive term, but this comes about as a result of *"the Church's apostolic authority to commission"* (Seminarian), and a belief that what is called *"the authority of gifts, should be with priests and bishops."* (Seminarian) The importance of organisational structures is evident to those who take a rather poor view of human nature. As one parish priest put it:

> *"Lay people with an axe to grind are no better than a similarly placed priest. People are still the same whether you put a collar on them or not. Human nature remains the same, and we need structures. The trouble with partnership is that you have to have two equal parts, and this is why it doesn't work."*

The inequality between lay people and priests is strengthened by a view which echoes the last quotation and implies on the part of the laity an inferior grasp of the nature of the Church:

> *"A lay Pope would be worse than an ordained Pope because lay people treat the Church as if it was a lay organisation, and the Church runs on totally different lines... Lay people can do most of the things we do as regards administration, but the Church does not like things on committee lines: it wants someone to be responsible."* (Non-parochial)

a qualified attitude towards lay dissent

Such a contrast has more to do with a stereotype than an appreciation of secular organisations. Those influenced by the orientation we are considering in this section take a qualified attitude towards lay dissent. It can be qualified by consideration of motive on both sides, as it were:

> *"It is important to understand the motives of those who challenge the faith. Disputes should be adjudicated impartially. Some forms of dissent have been handled badly because people get frightened."* (Seminarian)

It can also be qualified in terms of perception of likely consequences:

> *"The Church rarely canonises anyone who got on well with the hierarchy. The Church realises that the prophetic role and the administrative role are going to be in conflict. There cannot be

dissent from the Gospel. The law does not always clearly correspond to a particular situation, but if we endlessly proclaim the exceptions to the law people become confused." (Parish priest)

The reference to the Gospel demonstrates also the third qualification to support for loyal dissent, namely the status of the teaching to which dissent may be directed. So, one parish priest is unhappy with dissent from what he described generally as *"anything infallible"*, but another pointed to implicit problems of interpretation. He was adamant about his crucial official teaching role:

"I'm a priest. People don't want to come and hear my personal views, but the view of the Catholic Church and I have an obligation to give them." He continued, however, by drawing attention to a comparable obligation *"to interpret them to help people"*.

In relation to controversial issues facing the Church a functional/organisational view supports an attitude of acceptance of what is considered current teaching plus a willingness to accept change if that is what the Church decided. So, clerical celibacy is not viewed as of the essence of priesthood, but as an issue of discipline or as part of the package that has to be accepted given present teaching. Teaching on women priests is again broadly accepted, but a more open attitude to discussion is desirable. Acceptance can also be an attitude adopted to the real life situation of divorced Catholics who re-marry and come to communion.

a willingness to accept change

"The sacraments are not a reward for being good; they are given as a means, though they must not be abused or trivialised. The idea that the divorced and re-married coming to communion causes scandal has been overplayed. I have never refused the sacrament to anyone but drunks. If they [the divorced and re-married] ask before they come, then it's difficult." (Parish priest)

Communitarian Priest and open Church

An open Church incorporates a positive attitude towards the idea of loyal dissent.

> "It is looked on unfavourably, but is a healthy sign that the Church is living." (Non-parochial)

> "Loyal dissent has a very important place. Sometimes the Church has the wrong ideas, sometimes they are incomplete. It is important that we achieve some level of truth people can accept, a truth that has some authority. It does not harm to be challenged." (Non-parochial)

> "You have to live with dissent. Dissent can be an engine of change." (Parish priest)

> "It is part of the way we grow." (Recently ordained)

a more open approach

It also favours advocating a more open approach to the controversial issues facing the Church, and a greater appreciation of the ecumenical dimension.

So, in relation to clerical celibacy one parish priest said that the matter should be open to development, and that it should be regarded as an open issue. He believed that the question of the ordination of women was entirely a matter for the magisterium but that it needed to be addressed urgently. A non-parochial priest was concerned that a great many priests would not discuss celibacy. He went on to argue against the importance of Church structures if authority was to come into its own:

> "If the Church is to regain authority this won't come from structures but the internal evidence of what it is saying. A real authority is an author and an author stands on what he says, not on some external authority. If the Church claims ultimate authority from God, it must presume that God speaks to everybody from inside. The Church's authority should mirror or run parallel to conscience."

'speaking from the inside'

Such *'speaking from the inside'* is reflected in the value placed on experience in openness to the ecumenical dimension. So, the declaration of the invalidity of Anglican orders is judged primarily in terms of its likely reception by Anglicans:

> "Their orders can be valid but in a different way than the Catholic Church. Their understanding is not necessarily

> *sacrificial. We should not turn round to the Anglicans and say my orders are more valid than yours. To say that Anglican orders are invalid is hurting that community."* (Seminarian)

> *"When I worked with Anglicans I found that not much separates us... The Anglicans have their own valid ministry and their orders are valid in their own discipline."* (Recently ordained)

He had in fact received communion from an Anglican precisely because he *"felt to be in communion with those people."*

Openness is also evident in the attitude towards admitting the divorced and remarried to communion. One former priest argued as follows:

> *"There should be temporary exclusion if there is some good reason. The sacraments are not there for people who have passed the exam."*

A seminarian reflected that Christ should not be denied to anyone. A non-parochial priest took the view that:

> *"The only people who can be refused are those conscious of being in a state of serious sin. I think a lot of the divorced and remarried are free to receive. If we had taught the principles properly people would not be looking to priests, even the Pope, to make their minds up for them. The Church often goes on about scandal, but most people think that the scandal is that they are not allowed to receive."*

Placing the priest in the midst of community rather than set apart or as functioning in an organisational Church opens up a particular use of the priesthood.

> *"To me it's not a special role. It's no better nor worse than for a normal Christian."* (Seminarian)

> *"At the end of the day he has to be a priest for the people... It doesn't mean to me authority or prestige or power. It means working and living alongside people in their joys and their sorrows in the name of Christ."* (Recently ordained)

priest in the midst of community

> *"People still expect a lot from their priests... there is sometimes a tendency for people to expect the priest to have all the answers but that is totally untrue... Priests are just ordinary people with ordinary lives like anyone else."* (Seminarian)

> *"I have no ten year plan. I'm trying to bring about a community that knows one another, a community of faith and of love and hope and happiness, that grieves when it has to, which is endlessly led by the Spirit to answer the needs of the moment. It is for me to respond."* (Parish priest)

This perspective allows both for scope for lay people to play a special part in the discernment of vocation, and for choice of the priest as the only way to create change. The role of lay people in the selection of candidates is valued – and one parish priest wondered how he could have been appointed when the parish knew nothing of him – but a recently ordained priest saw a calling as coming not from the institutional Church but from ordinary people saying he would make a good priest. A respondent no longer in the priestly ministry recalled how:

> *"When I became a Catholic I thought the Catholic Church was in the front line of the defence of humanity. I realised a lay Catholic could do nothing. The only way to be of any influence was to be a priest."*

In the perspective considered in this final section the dividing line between priests and lay people becomes blurred.

> *"The priest is **merely** there for building the other members of the community, to enable them to exercise their common priesthood more fully."* (Seminarian)

> *"Many priestly functions are performed by lay people."* (Non-parochial)

> *"It is also suggested that lay people possess spiritual gifts."*
> (Resigned)

> *"Lay people can be spiritual directors, prayer leaders by **right** [emphasis original] from baptism, not by permission."* (Parish priest)

Another parish priest considered that lay people as baptised had a never-ending series of roles to play. A non-parochial priest thought that there was:

> "Very little the laity could not do. Sometimes I can claim to speak on behalf of the Church in a way that the individual lay person could not, though we might be saying exactly the same things."

The official function becomes residual, not central.

Those influenced by this perspective see the problem facing the Church less in terms of loss of faith and more in terms of the many cultures confronting the Church, and the challenge in inculturation. They also place the papacy not at the centre, but at the periphery of the Church, as a kind of symbol of unity, far away.

Perhaps this third orientation is best understood as practical, and some including the author whose work was cited at the beginning of this study have seen this as the essence of religion.

> "Religion and the religious consciousness, as I understand them, are essentially practical. A religion, in a manner to which philosophy is not subject, may be proved lacking by being proved inadequate to the demands of the ordinary life of ordinary people. Our felt wants are, of necessity, the starting point of **our** religion; not the complex desires of that kind of sophistication which would see clearly the nature and meaning of the universe as a whole, but the simple needs inseparable from an active and practical life."
> (Oakeshott, 1928)

the demands of ordinary life

Or as a character in **Our Game** by John le Carré put it *"We're religious – but no so religious we aren't secular"*.

This study has been constructed on the basis of lengthy conversations with those preparing for or immersed in the practice of priesthood, and with a small number of those chosen to have special responsibility for priests. The limitations of our work have been frankly acknowledged, but recognition should be given to the ways in which the study illuminates notions which must at least form part of the ongoing arguments within the Church. Perhaps the most striking finding is simply the plurality of view. Arguments may be only partially formed, but one of the main questions now facing the Church is how difference is experienced and lived with. This theme is taken up in the theological reflections that follow. Kenneth Wilson places priesthood in an essentially God-given world, expressing curiosity that none of those interviewed saw priesthood as a crucial societal function. Paul Conroy believes that the differences can be positively contained within the idea of tensions that must be experienced and borne.

Chapter Eight

THE AUTHORITATIVE CHURCH – THEOLOGICAL REFLECTIONS
Rev. Dr. KENNETH WILSON

The context

THE CHURCH PROCLAIMS the presence with God's world of God's enduring love. The instantiation of this is the transforming life and work of Jesus Christ that the Church celebrates in word, sacrament and service. Since God's love is forever present in and for the creation, the Church is the sign of God's love, not the means whereby it is secured let alone earned. She is thus called by God in Christ to bear witness to God's love and, in a world that knows much pain, to embody notwithstanding the possible suffering, the always-delightful life of love. The Church is indeed to be the Body of Christ. The Church presents the creation to God in her offering of worship and praise, and endeavours to bring the whole world to 'see' the Christ and to be embraced by his enlivening love. The fulfilment of this continuing vocation will always fluctuate between confidence and despair and tend to provoke personal anxiety and institutional tension. The Church in the Isles of Britain at the beginning of the twenty-first century is flustered by the experience of failure, tortured by suspicion and dishonour, pilloried by the media, which enjoys the spectacle of the notorious priest and the hypocritical layperson. No wonder therefore that there is real concern about the way forward, and in particular questions about the authority of the church, its nature and the exercise of it.

God's loving presence

This study is significant because of what it tells us about the self-perception of the Church in the world as at present experienced in the United Kingdom. The report focuses upon some of those who are or have been most intimately involved by reason of their office in exercising authority, namely Bishops, parish priests and religious, and former priests. However, there lies behind their comments the experience of the Church as a whole, many members of which rightly or wrongly seriously question whether the Church has the authority that it claims.

views of those in office

Theology and Ecclesiology

Indeed, at first sight, the interesting dimension of this enquiry is not the faith question, 'Does God have authority', but the ecclesiological question, 'Does the Church have authority?' While both questions seem to me to be answered in the affirmative, the latter is answered in such a way as to raise many serious issues. Moreover the answers highlight the essential ambiguity of the questions. The Church may have been given authority through its calling by Christ, but whether it possesses authority depends greatly upon the way in which it embodies and exercises it. All those involved in the Report understand that the authority of the Church is as a matter of fact being questioned: they differ on what the significance of this is and therefore on the response which should or could be made. On reflection, however, the most radical interpretation of the evidence would lead us to recognise that since in the minds of very many the authority of the Church and the authority of God are confused, rejection of the authority of the Church has also led to the rejection of the authority of God which is tantamount to the rejection of God. Hence the enquiry is of critical importance to faith and our understanding of God not simply to our understanding of the Church. We can see how intimately the two are bound in together for Christians; the Church is no optional extra, or a mere organisational support.

God and the Church

A long history

It is true of course that we are dealing with an age-old problem: authority has always been questioned. Many of the greatest movements in the Church, including for example many of the religious orders, have come about as a result of the questioning of authority and the way it has been expressed. As a result we can see that debate about the nature of authority – where authority lies – can be and very often has been positively constructive for human well-being. Indeed even a cursory reading of the New Testament itself provides evidence of justified debate about authority amongst the disciples themselves and in the emerging Church that leads to clarification with subsequent new opportunities for faith and understanding.[1]

'The supreme difficulty of our age has been the shaking of the foundations, so that no one seems quite sure what things that cannot be shaken remain. All authority has been questioned, and moral as well as intellectual confusion has doubtless ensued.'[2] This was written in 1901 by John Oman a Presbyterian scholar: it could be paralleled today in most traditions, and in secular as well as religious contexts. It underlines the importance of theology. But even there we must understand that there are no 'things that cannot be shaken'. For the fact that this is so we must thank God. It means that we can acquire knowledge precisely because all claims for truth can be tested. Of course, not all claims for truth can be tested in the same way. Whether or not the stallholder gave me the right change depends upon many things, whether I understood what the price was, whether the stallholder knew how much money I had given him and whether the stallholder and I could count properly, to name but three. When it comes to testing the truth of God in his revelation in Christ, the community of faith provides, not the only, but the critical context. If in that divine and human society I do not have my faith sustained, my awareness of God's love encouraged, my understanding extended, my curiosity aroused, and my desire to serve others stimulated, then at the very least my willingness to accept the authority of the Church will be questioned. And, from the ecumenical context in which I stand, I would have to say, rightly questioned. If authority cannot be questioned, on what can we depend for that priceless God-given human privilege, 'the advancement of learning', and growth in faith and understanding.

All is in flux?

Growth in faith and understanding

There is more to it than this.

'Authority is a fact of social life. Most often it is simply accepted. When abused, it turns into authoritarianism. Although authoritarian regimes can reign for a long time, societies seldom thrive under them. Eventually those kept subservient react to such authority. The desire for freedom, when smothered by authoritarianism, sometimes manifests itself in the opposite extreme – anarchism. Societies seldom thrive under conditions of anarchy either, nor are such conditions stable and long-lived.'[3] Nowhere is this truer than when considering authority in relation to the Church. By its very nature the Church is a community because it is the Body of Christ. There are duties and responsibilities that flow from this fact. However, the gospel of Jesus Christ is a gospel of freedom. We must of course understand freedom in the context of faith. Freedom is not a licence to do anything whatsoever provided

Authority and freedom

only that one felt inclined to do it; that would be anarchy. Nobody believes that the freedom of the gospel is anarchic. However, it is also true that the freedom of the gospel is not determined by what others 'in authority' permit those 'under authority' to do. On the contrary the freedom of all the baptised comes from intelligent consideration of the relevant evidence in the light of scripture and tradition as interpreted by the people of God, the Church. It is therefore the task of the Church, the people of God, in its various structures and many-sided life not only to safeguard human freedom, but to enhance it. Any move on the part of the Church towards authoritarian structures will deny its nature, frustrate this possibility and therefore prevent others from seeing the Christ whose Body she is. Authoritarianism makes unlovable the very God whose love is the source of our being, and whose purpose is to give us abundant life.

Obscuring or revealing?

It is very apparent from the NOP Report that many are concerned that the Church may be behaving in a way that obscures rather than reveals the God who called her into being; indeed some are sure that it is so. They believe that the Church may appear to others to love herself rather than God as revealed in Christ. They fear that the Church has focused upon herself rather than God. They are concerned that fear of the world as we are beginning to build it through science and technology with all its opportunities and challenges, will result in the Church venturing little and losing her soul. Love of God and love of the Church therefore bring such people to look for and work for reform, for change, for the possibility of development. While clearly not everything that the world wants is good, the richness of the opportunities are God-given and it is up to us mere human beings to discern what is good and embody it.

Change or re-affirmation?

Others are more content with things as they are and see things very differently. For these it is a case of, 'if only the Church and all her orders would accept authority and get on with living life appropriately, everything would be all right'. It is not that we have new opportunities, about which to make choices, but that we have been disobedient to the heavenly vision as instantiated in scripture and interpreted in the tradition. Thus it is disobedience that is the root cause of the Church's apparent failure, and compromise with those of a liberal disposition that lies behind her continuing difficulties. What is wanted is a thoroughly clear and convincing assertion of the truth, moral, intellectual, theological and an abrogation of all forms of 'dialogue' or 'debate'. We know what to say, but we have lost our nerve to say it clearly and to ask for obedience to it. Love of God and love of the Church will therefore cause such people to want to tighten the reins and accept this time as a period of testing for the Church. The Church may contract, it will certainly be misunderstood, but the experience only fulfils scriptural truth and the teaching of tradition. The Church cannot fail if it remains faithful.

In conversation?

It is important to affirm that what is taking place in the interviews is conversation, not a confrontation. Therefore we, and all those who took part, have the possibility of learning. There is little if any aggression in the engagements. Moreover as one reflects on the material one is drawn to the conclusion that we need and should enjoy the strength of many of the perspectives. All need to be drawn into the conversation. The priest who sees himself as serving the community at large needs to be a parish manager or he will find himself with little to celebrate and no congregation on whom he can rely to work with him in serving the community. Moreover if he does not celebrate the fact of God's presence with God's people in word and sacrament, he will soon lose his awareness of the ground of his being and come falsely to rely on himself and his managerial skill. We need them all. The danger is that the personality of the priest may lead him to opt for one and to reject the others and to respond to his experience in such a way as to confirm the prejudice inherent in his personality. What is more given the authority of the priest which, amongst the members of the parish will of course be much greater than the authority of the Church in the world, it is his conversation which will be likely to influence disproportionately the wider conversation of the parish.

For the priest whose experience is almost entirely limited to the tradition in which he was born, or whose Christian life is coterminous with his life in the Catholic Church, it will naturally be very difficult to entertain the thought that the conversation could or need be any larger. Thus amongst those interviewees who

Conversation with all

The role of the priest

were still active in their priestly vocation, there is less interest in eucharistic hospitality, and the validity of Anglican Orders than in the possibility of married clergy and the admittance of divorced persons and married persons in mixed marriages to communion. The latter must after all take up a far greater share of conversation amongst Bishops and priests than the former because they concern a large and growing number of Catholics. Everyone knows that the number of vocations is falling; almost everyone must know several persons who are distressed by the discipline that rules that on only very rare occasions may even a faithful Christian married to a Catholic be admitted to receive communion. The fact that both eucharistic hospitality and the validity of Anglican Orders is more likely to gain the support of priests who have resigned may be due to their greater familiarity with the ecumenical situation. The wider Christian community may figure more prominently in their conversation.

The role of the Curia and the freedom of the Bishop in Ordinary

Many respondents expressed concern about the question of the exercise of authority by the Curia. This is not surprising. One might think that the Bishop in Ordinary is the authority in his diocese. Of course, in principal that is the case. However, the Bishop is also directly involved in conversation with the Curia and the Pope. Whereas an individual priest may be able 'to live and let live', sheltered perhaps by the judicious style of his Bishop and the conversation of his parish and fellow parish priests, the Bishop himself is bound to be aware of the constraints of hierarchical pressure. He may likewise be frustrated or made anxious by the difficulties that arise in the contemporary world when one law, or more especially one interpretation of the law is made to cover all cases and every diocese. So for example when there is a statement from the Curia to the effect that further discussion of the ordination of women is forbidden, many Bishops may wonder what on earth that means. Does the Curia understand the local context in which this conversation is taking place in each diocese? How exactly is such a rule to be implemented? Is it enough if the Bishop does not encourage such conversation and refrains from putting it on the agendas of diocesan conferences? Does it cover communications between individuals on the Internet or only statements that have been published? And what exactly does 'publishing' mean anyway given the changes in technology?

Moreover does it mean the same in Rwanda as it does in The Netherlands or Peru? The importance of contextualisation is profound: without an awareness of its significance, unnecessary conflict may be provoked. Bishops want to fulfil their vocations as pastor pastorum, celebrants, preachers and teachers; but without the support of Church authority – which means the Church Authorities – they will lack the freedom to do so. What sort of authority do the Church Authorities think they are exercising or asking Bishops to exercise, when they make declarations of this kind? One might say that Bishops depend for their authority on being able to talk with anybody about anything. Small wonder if some bishops in different parts of the world are concerned about the curtailment of their authority.[4] The more complex the world becomes the more sensitive and discriminating an authority is likely to have to be if it is to be authoritative. This truth applies to ecclesiastical structures as to all others: the fact of revelation only underlines the essential significance of this responsibility.

contextualisation

Complexity and authority

The role of the laity, and in particular the role of women, in the Church is an intriguing question. The Laity have authority, and therefore women have authority too. Their authority does not depend upon priestly authority, but their freedom to be authoritative does. Yet in order to determine and secure the special status of the authority of the priest there is a great deal of language under-pinning its apartness, and in effect, its centrality. How is this to be understood? Given that the focus of conversation in the formation of the priest is largely other intending priests, priests, together with scripture, theology and the liturgy, it is to be expected that the priest will acquire a language that separates his experience and thus his conversation from that of the ordinary parishioner, let alone those of the population at large. The same could be said of course of the mathematician or technician; he or she will focus upon the material of the discipline for a substantial part of the time. However, the latter acquire their knowledge and skills in a community where other interests and dimensions of life flourish with which they can engage, whereas the priest is denied this. The world of the priest's formation is confined and limited. Whatever argument may be presented in favour of this, it will almost inevitably tend to result in a restricted sympathy of conversation and the self-referencing of criteria of judgement

including the laity in the conversation

151

when faced with difficulty or the need for new judgements. Indeed, the later isolation of many a priest in the fastness of the presbytery will be likely to exaggerate the isolation by lack of conversation, even contact with other priests.

The priest in the Church

Certainly the stance of the priests involved in the report seems to be that of the servant of Christ, and of the People of God which may ambiguously be said to include not only those within the Church but in principle all people. Hardly any for example took seriously the thought that the priesthood should be regarded as a profession set apart. There is no concern with status for the priest but rather a concern with the status of all people, provided only that due significance was given to the status of priesthood. To bring people into a proper relationship with God through Christ and His Church is they believed the only way to do this. Whether seminarian, priest (both parochial and non-parochial), or a priest who has resigned, all seem to want quite unselfconsciously to work towards this end. The signs may not be very good, but it is possible for them on the whole to remain hopeful for the Church, but only because of their prior faith in God and the belief that God will not – indeed cannot – let his Church down by abandoning her to the depredations of human insensitivity and indifference.

The priest in the world

I think, however, that it is remarkable that no respondent referred to the wide societal functions which priesthood might perform. The almost exclusive focus of the priest on the Church, to the apparent exclusion of the world where, on sound theological grounds, it must also be affirmed that God is present seems strange. Surely the Catholic position is that the Church is God's gift to the world for the world's sake: conversion involves making the scales fall from the eyes of the believer who may therefore be freed to see the goodness of God's creation, as well as bringing the sinner to repentance that he may know God's grace. If this is so, as I believe it to be, then the focus of the priest upon those who are called 'the People of God' means that the Church in the world depends upon the authority with which the laity fulfils its own calling. Not that this can be done, or even be thought of in isolation for at whatever point the Church is, there is present the whole Church. But this means that for the laity to act with authority in their calling depends upon the way the Authorities are perceived, and the extent to which they act in order to support and the develop the freedom of the believer. Hence the frustration when the Church does not appear to hear, let alone to pay due attention to, the word of the expert, or so to limit the contexts in which expert voices are heard as to disenfranchise the majority who are experts. The classic case is artificial contraception and the putting aside of medical, psychological and sociological expertise in the process of making a decision emphasised again in the United Nations Cairo Conference on Population Control in 1996. But the question is far wider. It is encouraging that in what might be regarded as safer areas, for example cosmology and community development, there is much evidence of a more generous perspective. Even in regard to the very difficult and fraught matter of relationships with other faiths, there is reason to believe that serious work is under way. The point is that conversation is encouraged and not precluded by prior decision in the absence of evidence. This process will undoubtedly take some time to reach the public consciousness even of the majority of the faithful. However, the approach of virtually all interviewed for this report supports the view that nothing should be excluded from the conversation of faith, for if it is well founded, the conversation will undoubtedly be strengthened rather than threatened. On these grounds one might also be optimistic about the confidence that will come to be shown by making room for the laity (including women!) in the fullest possible way in the conversation of the Church. However, it seems that notwithstanding the willingness of the priest to encourage the laity to serve the Church in those capacities where the priest acknowledges either ignorance or incompetence, namely finance, administration and interestingly marriage instruction, some further shocks may be necessary before the whole lay experience of the secular world is allowed to feed into the theological understanding and ecclesiastical practice.

Working towards the 'wholeness' of our human conversation in the Faith

The ecumenical scene

The ecumenical scene has changed dramatically over the last century. In my childhood I was told stories of Protestant children in Liverpool at the beginning of the century being urged by their parents to cross the road when they saw a catholic priest in case he was carrying his 'magic' box and cast his spell over them. I was not told this approvingly, but as an example of how things had changed

A new ecumenism

by the nineteen fifties. By then the Churches had been involved in a conversation that had led to the establishment of the World Council of Churches in 1948 at Amsterdam. Even if the Roman Catholic Church was not formally a member of it, she was 'in attendance'. The point is that the conversation then begun has continued, and extended both in range and in depth.

As far as the United Kingdom is concerned what was the British Council of Churches in which the Roman Catholic Church had observer status, has become the Council of Churches in Britain and Northern Ireland, of which the Roman Catholic Church is a constituent member. Moreover we have moved from a position where we might rightly have talked of an Ecumenical Movement, to an ecumenical scene in which we look for piecemeal development via bilateral conversations, the publishing of agreed reports, and the nourishing of communities of Christians for significant conversation locally. The Ecumenical Movement began when the Churches realised at the turn of the nineteenth and twentieth centuries that population expansion was facing each separated Church with an impossible missionary problem, and that there were social, political and moral issues on which it was vital that they should work together, – as far as was possible. Now, it seems to me, we have arrived at a time when we recognise that however generous and gracious the perception, unity is not a means to an end but the only way in which Christ's Church can invite the world to 'see' God and become free to be his loving disciples. There is something organic about 'Church' which means that the Churches can never allow themselves to give up the quest for the unity which is in accordance with God's will. The question of authority in the Church is a vital ingredient in this matter. It is also, if unavoidable, nevertheless a matter of the greatest complexity and difficulty.

The report, of course, focuses upon the nature and experience of authority as perceived by those most intimately involved in its exercise: the ecumenical scene is not taken into account except when it comes to the consideration of the problems occasioned by Anglican orders, and the questions for eucharistic discipline provided by inter-church marriages and divorced persons. However, there are pointers that are both encouraging and disturbing.

On the one hand, there is evidence of sympathetic understanding that the consequences of Church division need to be attended to in so far as they work out in the lives of families and local communities. We have to find a way forward. Credibility and therefore authority is at stake. On the other hand, there is no sense, apparently, that if these are to be done honestly and in such a way as to invite acceptance of the authority of the Church, much more is required than a reform of private pastoral practice. Furthermore, it is important that the Pope has invited sister Churches to reflect with Him on the nature of the Papal Office and how it might exercise authority in such a way as to invite their future co-operation and support. All Christians would welcome an ecumenical development that meant that the Faith had one voice in the world, as far as it is possible and desirable. However, the fact that bishops, his primary partners in the conversation of faith were not invited themselves to express an opinion on the matter is inclined to encourage disquiet. As I noted above, it is not a coincidence that the bishops who carry the greatest responsibility should find themselves least comfortable with the way the Curia often chooses to act.

The Papal Office

It is often said that the Roman Catholic Church is not, and never could be a democratic organisation. I am not sure why this should be so vigorously asserted when the evolution of our understanding of democracy is so rapid, and when centralisation of power is so obviously not always consistent with the willing acceptance or understanding of authority. However, putting that on one side, the conditions of the contemporary world which none of us can baulk, do seem to require that if authority is to be accepted it must involve inclusive conversation. It will take a long time for this to become the case. However, the process has begun. From this point of view, the calling of Vatican II with all that has involved in respect of consultation, prayer, theological enquiry and publication marked, and still marks, a critical point. The report points to many ways in which the conversation between traditions, between religions, and with the world is gaining impetus. As it grows, so will the authority of the Church that encourages it.

Becoming authoritative

The most important fact to come out of the study is the wide range of views contained within the Church, and the unity that holds it all together. There is clearly a hard row to hoe, but it can be done in such a way as to bring freedom, confidence and hope not only to the Church, but also to the world. It will be helped by the inclusiveness of the conversation, and that depends upon the desire for it. One could simply bury the talent one has; it would of course be better to seek the pearl of great price notwithstanding the digging, and hard, painful work which will be required.

Kenneth Wilson
Director of Research, The Queen's Ecumenical Foundation for Theological Education

---

[1] For example, the debate over the authority of the Torah amongst the disciples of Jesus, and the nature of the apostolate as it affected the relationship between Peter and Paul.

[2] John Oman, Vision and Authority, London, Hodder & Stoughton, 1902, p. 1. The subtitle 'The Throne of St. Peter' is significant given the period when the book was written and the Presbyterian tradition of the author, who later became (1925-35) the Principal of Westminster College, Cambridge. Indeed Oman was convinced of the self-authenticating nature of religious experience while at the same time recognising the importance of putting this alongside other human experience. In so doing he knew he was raising the question of authority that in good Presbyterian style he saw as focused upon discipline. Thus the significance of the order of the four sections of this volume, 'The Internal Authority', 'The External Authority', 'The Church's Creed', 'The Church's Organisation'.

[3] Richard T de George, The Nature and Limits of Authority, Lawrence, University of Kansas Press, 1985, p. 1. This philosophical work is focused upon political authority, but includes substantial useful discussion of authority as it effects religion. See Part 3, chapter 10, pp. 217-243. Interestingly, and appropriately, this chapter precedes one on 'The University and Authority', for in both contexts and in analogous ways, the task of authority is to stimulate freedom.

[4] See for example chapter six 'The Reform of the Roman Curia' in Archbishop John R Quinn's book *The Reform of the Papacy* New York, The Crossroads Publishing Company 1999.

Chapter Nine

LIVING WITH TENSION
Fr. PAUL CONROY

IN MEASURE FOR MEASURE Shakespeare acknowledges, through Isabella, that the abuse of authority is an easy fault for human beings. This is a complex matter, however, for its abuse is often the consequence of being sure of something we hardly know at all.

> "Man proud man,
> Dress'd in a little brief authority,
> Most ignorant of what he's most assur'd,
> His glassy essence, like an angry ape,
> Plays such fantastic tricks before high heaven
> As makes the angels weep."[1]

In Measure for Measure, of course, the zeal of the Authority which Isabella initially seeks to temper develops, as the story unfolds, into corruption. What lies behind many of the experiences that are recounted in this study is a considerable degree of zeal. Mercifully, I do not see signs of deliberate corruption.

Nevertheless, I believe we have come to understand that accountability is in the first place the great bulwark against deliberate corruption. It also provides, however, a challenge to hypocrisy, which is a more insidious and subtle form of corruption, of the self-serving kind. Thankfully, we have become generally more sensitive towards and less tolerant of hypocrisy. Self-examination in a moral and spiritual sense is important for the health of the whole person and anything that promotes health is good. This study offers the occasion for priests in particular and those in positions of authority in general to recall their duty to undertake the sometimes painful duty of examining ourselves. The compilers of the report are satisfied that the method used to produce it and the insights it offers give a good point of reference and presumably would be happy to offer it as an instrument in this work of self-examination.

The survey, carried out through a number of conversations, may also suggest a model for self-examination that can achieve a degree

accountability and self-examination through conversation

of accountability. If through dialogue we open our attitudes, values and actions to the concerned scrutiny of others, we demonstrate in a very real way a willingness to find out the truth, to ensure that it is the truth we are living by and correct anything that needs to be corrected.

If the survey does indeed suggest a model for self-examination and accountability, it is also to be hoped that the rich data it has gathered can be studied further. Since the study contains much that is painful and some things that are critical, there is a danger that it will be abused as a stick with which to beat the backs of those who are and have been responsible for the exercise of authority and governance in the Roman Catholic Church. It could easily be perceived as an exercise in negativity by priests and bishops, especially if some of the painful or critical things are exploited by the media or anyone with an axe to grind. An atmosphere of vulnerability surrounds the survey as a whole as well as the men who took part in it and by extension all of us who are linked to it by association. The pain felt by those who have resigned from the ministry or religious life is easily identified. Underlining this are some of the accounts of unsympathetic treatment from those in authority both at the time of resignation and subsequently.

a vulnerability that leads to conversion

The ability and willingness to weigh up what is voiced is crucial and although the ability is not lacking the willingness may be a problem. The Church is not accustomed to being perceived publicly as vulnerable. It is having to become used to it. There is however, no point in vulnerability for vulnerability's sake – it has to produce results; in this case, it might be hoped, a deeper conversion to the Gospel and a more effective witness to the Reign of God.

One of the things that the survey lays bare is the existence of opposing views among those interviewed. Part of the vulnerability surrounding the survey is having to account for this conflict. Tolerance is one response to the discomfort caused by the conflict that results when opposing views meet. Tolerance can sometimes be an escape from tension. It may not, therefore, be an altogether honest response for it often brings premature closure to the worthwhile ambition of taking hold of the truth.

The discovery of the truth is usually brought about when the tension of inquiry aroused by the conflict ends. However, even when the conditions are right, it sometimes requires great moral courage to embrace the truth when one is confronted by it. Confrontation is not a congenial environment in which to let go of one's deeply felt opinions. It is not unknown for truth to challenge our more cherished prejudices, what we have taken all along for truth and a way of serving the truth. A more respectful situation can make the letting go easier.

A more respectful situation and a more honest response to conflict is dialogue – the kind of conversation, perhaps, that took place in the course of the NOP survey we are considering. It is unlikely that any hoped for continuation of the dialogue and the conversations that have already taken place would be likely without being provoked by the various tensions out of which they seem to have arisen. It may not be unrealistic to hope that a continuation of the dialogue will provide benefits that go beyond being merely resolutions to the tensions they initially set out to address. A whole new way of doing things might result.

dialogue as a sign of respect for the truth

Those who engage in dialogue, if they do so honestly, must be willing to accept that their conclusions so far, either theological or existential might be wrong or at least might need to be corrected. This goes for those who are regarded traditionally as the exercisers of authority as well as those who from time to time take issue with the conclusions reached as well as with the way authority has been exercised. Respect for the truth also requires that we accept that it can sometimes happen that it is the truth that is being upheld even when the means of doing so are suspect or those who do so seem less worthy of regard than those who oppose them.

In the rhetoric[2] of contemporary society, however, truth is not a significant unit of the currency. What appeals to much of contemporary taste resembles more the Sophistry of ancient Greece, against which Socrates, Plato and Aristotle in particular toiled. The categories of traditional and liberal, right and left wing, while providing a certain degree of convenience for present day commentators are perhaps less than helpful in a consideration of the broad sweep of views, many of them not inherently consistent.

159

As the study reveals, alongside the anecdotal, there is a great deal of emotion in what has been related. And while our emotions undoubtedly have something to tells us about the present situation it would, I believe, be a mistake to be left with the impression that they alone provide an adequate or comprehensive hermeneutic.

Like much of the rest of society the Church is prone to the *"knee-jerk reaction"*. When something happens the response is often reflex – a defensive reply to a perceived attack. In the first Encyclical letter of his pontificate Paul VI seemed to propose an attitude that would consign this way of behaving to the past.[3] In section 3 especially, speaking of dialogue, this letter lays great store by the ability through dialogue to arrive at a truly profound understanding and experience of the truth. Yet strangely, although the conciliar documents themselves are for the most part clear attempts to promote dialogue in this way, there are many examples of a different approach holding sway in the post-conciliar Church.

spirituality of the priest and poverty, chastity and obedience

As readers will know, the NOP survey draws data from a number of lengthy conversations. When I came to consider the issues raised in the conversations I found myself drawn towards the words poverty, chastity and obedience. These terms are scarcely mentioned as such in the survey and are seldom found in the rhetoric. They are, however, *"classical"* terms, sometimes referred to as the *"evangelical counsels"* and have tended to be associated with religious life, identifying the three vows taken by religious men and women at their profession. Understood as a sign of personal commitment to the life-style of the order or congregation of which he or she is becoming a member, they are also given some importance in Vatican II's account of the spirituality of the priest.[4]

One of the recurring themes drawn out of the NOP survey is the absence of or at least widespread confusion surrounding what might be termed the *"spirituality"* of the priest. Given the importance attached to poverty, chastity and obedience by the Vatican II document, I want to consider whether there is any real chance that these classical terms will have meaning today, in the light of what the survey has shown. Is it possible that they might contribute to a deeper appreciation of the spirituality of the priest? Vatican II seemed to think they would. In fact, I too believe they do offer an interesting hermeneutic, by which I mean a key to interpret the events that are unfolding around us, and as the survey indicates, often absorbing us.

More and more I seem to hear people voicing their concern that the renewal of the Church envisaged by the Second Vatican Council is becoming a missed opportunity. It would not be the first time that the renewal that a Council seeks to inspire has been lost. Historians tell us that although the doctrinal aspects of the Council of Trent came to be well known and widely promoted, the pastoral renewal that was envisaged and provided for, for the most part did not happen. In the experience of many people Vatican II was about the liturgical reforms. For the vast majority of people the ecclesiological and spiritual renewal that this should have come to express has never been appreciated. I include in this vast majority of people a large number of priests and others who have been expected to lead the Church into this time of post-conciliar renewal. There is still time to ensure that the radical renewal required for the vision of Vatican II to take root will not be lost. However, that will require an ongoing commitment on the part of the leadership of the Church to their own personal renewal and conversion. Priests and bishops are not sufficiently aware of the *"spirituality of communion"* that Vatican II proposes. The thing about spirituality is that although it can be spoken about, written about and studied, it has to be lived. The shift that Vatican II proposes not only needs to take place in terms of a personal conversion but also requires a *"conversion of structures"*, changes in the organisational and institutional aspects of the Church's life that are needed to promote and support the new spirituality. Unless and until this happens it will be virtually impossible to have lived-experience of the spirituality of communion.

The discomfort that is at times evident in the survey between what priests say when they are theorising about *"priestly spirituality"* and their description of the practical pastoral approaches they take can, I think, be accounted for by the failure to commit both personally and institutionally to the demands of the conversion called for by Vatican II. There is little lived-experience of this spirituality around.

Although traditionally poverty, chastity and obedience have usually been associated with the vows taken by those who enter religious

Vatican II's vision of renewal

life, in fact the Vatican II document on the ministry and life of priests uses them as touchstones to speak of the special spiritual requirements in the life of the priest. They will only have value, however, if they can be rediscovered in the context of the renewal envisaged by Vatican II and the spirituality of communion.

spirituality of communion

Commentators on the Council have generally agreed that the document on the ministry and life of priests emerged as something of an afterthought. It is clear that great attention was paid to the new ecclesiology and to the ministry of bishops. Priests have always considered that they were given a raw deal. Nevertheless, by reading Presbyterorum Ordninis in the light of Lumen Gentium[5] and Gaudium et Spes[6] a new description of what we might understand by poverty, chastity and obedience can be proposed. The failure of most of those who took part in the survey to make any reference to poverty, chastity and obedience is due, I believe, to a lack of experience, personally and institutionally, of the spirituality of communion that these counsels are capable of promoting and helping us to develop.

membership of a movement of volunteers

However, before moving on to look at this in more detail, I want to comment on an idea that struck me from Professor Kerkhofs' foreword. In speaking of the Church he says it is *"neither a business, nor a bank nor an army. It is first of all a movement of volunteers. At all levels the members should treat one another as volunteers, putting their gifts of body and mind into the growth of this movement, where the Spirit of the Lord is the principal leader."*

I would suggest that the word *"movement"* is not a familiar part of church rhetoric in England, Wales or Scotland. Perhaps it has overtones of the pseudo-religious political movements in parts of Europe in the 30's and 40's of the last century. *"Membership"* also, at least in Scotland, tends to be a term more commonly used by the Church of Scotland. Even so, seeing these words together raises for me a question about our understanding of Christian Initiation. What is it we are becoming involved with when we are brought to the Eucharist through Baptism and Confirmation? Do we achieve membership, join a movement or something else? The notion of the Church as *"first of all a movement of volunteers"* has its appeal, and something of its appeal is described by Professor

Kerkhofs. To my mind, the freedom of the volunteer is one of the most attractive features, yet the effective volunteer very quickly finds freedom being channelled into commitment in the form of responsibilities and obligations. The volunteer remains out on a limb unless he or she joins with others to become part of a wider movement.

This brings me back to poverty, chastity and obedience. Although they take on an external manifestation, I believe they are essentially internal attitudes. They can, in fact, only be required of volunteers. In pointing out that the Spirit of the Lord is the principal leader of the Church, Professor Kerkhofs identifies its fundamentally charismatic nature. Yet the pursuit of poverty, chastity and obedience has been given a clear institutional purpose. Even the most charismatic of religious orders or congregations have, from time to time, found a value in a certain degree of institutionalisation, standing firm, as it sometimes has to do, against the tyranny of the zealot. The evangelical counsels become the hallmarks of a particular kind of institution – one whose volunteers seek freedom through commitment.

The spirituality of communion is proposed as the way to a vision of the daughters and sons of God enjoying freedom and fullness of life. The evangelical counsels of poverty, chastity and obedience are signs of the commitment of the *"volunteers"*. In considering the tensions faced by priests in particular in the exercise of their ministry, I will do so against the background of poverty, chastity and obedience insofar as I believe they are able to make concrete the spirituality of communion. Poverty proposes a lifestyle and a way of being community that is prophetic, credible and free. Chastity proposes a lifestyle and a way of being community that is respectful, trusting and responsible. Obedience proposes a lifestyle and a way of being community that carefully listens (to the word of God and the signs of the times) and responds with justice and love.

The reality we face is that we strain after these *"ideals"* in situations that are marked by the tension of what is *"already"* but *"not yet"*. The tensions reveal the different perspectives that need to be taken into account as we try to move towards our goal. The tensions remind us that we are never truly poor, truly chaste or truly obedient but have many opportunities to begin to experience the

the tension of the already but not yet

the charismatic and the institutional

spirituality of communion and glimpse something of the vision God has for his people.

One of the tensions that emerges for me from this survey is the tension between what is charismatic and what is institutional. I have already hinted at this tension in describing the attitude of dialogue proposed by Paul VI in his first encyclical and the more prescriptive approach taken by Church authorities in many documents and other interventions made since the Council. It goes without saying that the tension this describes is not a new discovery. What is worth mentioning, however, is that the principal locus of this tension is not to be found in those whose role in ministry might be perceived in the terms set out by Noel Timms — Sacred Priest and Closed Church: Priests as Functionaries in an Organisational Church: Communitarian Priest and Open Church. The tension between institutional and charismatic, prescriptive and dialogal is present in almost all of those interviewed because it is already present in the Church as a whole. The tension that these tendencies represent is an internal tension found in almost every priest, rather than the different ways individuals have tried to resolve the tension. Although one outlook might well be dominant in this or that priest, all priests are, I maintain, at one time or another Sacred or Functional or Communitarian, and what is more, expected to be so by those they serve.

The priest's vulnerability comes from having to live with, not to say within, this tension. Yet though this may be one of the great concerns, it is perhaps also one of the great strengths of priests today — for in some cases it certainly points to an ability, albeit in some cases the paralysing ability, to see the merits of a range of different points of view. Alongside what I have already described as the problems priests face in matching theory and practice, I believe that this ability could be considered to be part of the *"institutional culture"* of the priesthood.

Even if a particular priest might present one or other orientation in the extreme, his insertion into the body of priests in a diocese will sometimes lead to some kind of levelling out. This probably means there is a conservative ethos at work in almost every presbyterium and the levelling out virtually always means that change to what is better when it happens comes about only very slowly. Given the difficulties that the tensions we live with provoke, it is disturbing to find – not to say virtually impossible to work with – a priest who is totally and utterly convinced that all the answers are charismatic or all of them institutional. This cuts both ways for experience shows that saints are often impossible to live with and devils invariably disruptive.

questions and answers

Tension is, nonetheless, the inevitable consequence of hard questions and though it may not always be comfortable is it probably wise and realistic to accept, along with Bernard Lonergan, that the range of possible questions will always be larger than the range of possible answers (at least on this side of the grave).[7] None of us can expect to find all the answers. Furthermore – it may seem obvious to say it – the harder the question the more elusive the answer seems to be and the greater the tension the pursuit of an answer generates. This is not an excuse for giving up the pursuit but merely a recognition that in the short to medium term conversation and dialogue demand more time and energy than prescription and the closure it imposes, usually prematurely.

the priest as a man of virtue

What then, of poverty, chastity and obedience? There is a general expectation that the priest will be a person of virtue. This is evident in the New Testament but also in the tabloid newspapers. The latter set so much store by this that the failures and sins of priests (and bishops) are able to make the front pages. (Sadly, the sometimes heroic living out of these virtues is less frequently extolled.) Even if the rhetoric is different, the stories that grab the headlines as far as priests are concerned are to do with chastity, obedience and, to a lesser extent, poverty. Virtue, even in popular circles, appears to be measured by the extent to which a priest is faithful or unfaithful to the ideals proposed by these counsels.

Faced with the expectation that the priest will always be a man of virtue, the institution of the priesthood and the Church at large is judged according to the success or failure of each individual to match the expectations. When failure occurs those in authority become involved, frequently bringing to light an inexperience or naïvete of those in authority that is not rarely gleefully portrayed as incompetence or even disregard.

Ironically the experience of failure demonstrates that virtue has a community dimension. Everyone is touched even by the isolated incident of failure. On the one hand, everyone is tarred with the same brush. On the other hand the *"clamping down, tightening up"* reaction demonstrates a breakdown in trust. We suffer when those in authority do not seem to have the same understanding of or commitment to what is demanded as those they serve. Experience suggests that it is not always the person who seems to be stepping out of line who has failed to understand what is meant by these virtues or failed to be faithful to them. The truly virtuous person is also a free person and the meaning of and commitment to these virtues becomes lost if the freedom that they represent is not evident. Jesus Christ, after all was not one of the recognised leaders. Freedom meant he was able to admonish the authorities for loading intolerable burdens on others without lifting a finger to help.[8]

"Obedience" means first and foremost listening to God, and that, Catholic tradition acknowledges, can mean that those in authority are wrong. Noel Timms reminds us of the wisdom of St. Benedict who allowed in his Rule for the possibility that the youngest of the community would suggest a better course of action than the abbot. If the attention given to failure reflects the level of expectation, then the priest is certainly expected to be a person of virtue, not only by people of faith but by society as a whole. Traditionally these virtues are pursued by individuals in their personal quest for holiness. There is also, however, as I have already suggested, a way of considering them as institutional hallmarks of a virtuous society. If, as happens, the lapses and wrongdoing of individual members of the clergy reflect on the whole body, then surely it can also be said that the virtues of the majority accumulate until a generally virtuous climate is established. People, therefore, expect that priests will be obedient, chaste and sparing, and by and large that is what they find.[9]

poverty

It will be noted that I have already begun to interpret what is meant by the virtue of poverty. The whole community needs to learn in a new way the meaning of poverty. Presbyterorum Ordinis speaks of the importance of priests having *"a right attitude to the world and to earthly goods."*[10]

Personally I have always found the issue of poverty a challenging one. I am, therefore, surprised that is does not seem to have found more than a passing mention in the course of the survey of attitudes among priests. The poor are usually also the weak and are likely to be the most vulnerable when power is abused. Yet this does not seem to have been a concern. Some serious questions were asked about the administrative competence of priests and bishops but there seemed to have been more concern with efficient financial management than a questioning of how an apparently wealthy Church can proclaim a Gospel that is primarily destined for the poor.

This is one of the areas where I feel acutely the tension between what I have referred to as the charismatic and the institutional. The same number in Presbyterorum Ordinis announces that *"Priests are to manage ecclesiastical property ..."* and advises that *"priests are invited to embrace voluntary poverty."* The danger we face is the perpetuation of a dichotomy between the wealth of the institution and the poverty of the priest. I do not believe that anyone is called to be destitute, however, it takes great strength of character to find practical ways of embracing voluntary poverty while having the astuteness needed (albeit *"with the help, as far as possible of skilled lay people"*) in the present day and age to *"manage ecclesiastical property"*. I can use words like detachment and indifference all I like but they do not dispense me from the duty of self-examination to ensure that I am not stifling the Spirit out of my concern to be a prudent and wise steward in my Master's house.

I recall a priest telling me how people in one of the communities he served were outraged because the people in a neighbouring community had bought their priest a Mercedes Benz car, while he was going about on an old motorcycle. Their outrage was due to the fact that because he refused to consider driving around in such a car they would be given a showing up by their apparently more prosperous neighbours. The dependence on the people that marks the poverty of the priest can also become a form of abuse, for the priest can become domesticated and no longer prophetic, rather like a prize poodle whose well-being and life-style make it a symbol of its owner's success.

Few priests succumb to the temptation to become prize poodles. Some, in fact, live in the midst of poverty and themselves suffer hardship because of it. I have seen priests living in poverty. Fortunately I am not one of them. We do not choose to live in squalor or in situations of multiple deprivation as a gesture. However, the poverty of the Gospel – the right attitude to the world and to earthly goods – is capable of being an option showing solidarity with those who are truly poor. I am not sure, however, that we are a church of the poor. I don't know if it is possible to be a church of the poor without being a poor Church. Figures indicate that the gap between the wealthy and the poor is widening. What also seems to be the case is that the Church of the experience of most of us in the West finds itself less and less capable of identifying with the poor. This for me is one of the real issues to do with authority and governance in the Roman Catholic Church today, for if the concerns and preoccupations of the Church are considered to be no more than the concerns and preoccupations of people of wealth then there will be no possibility that the Church can remain in conversation with the poor, far less be able to identify with them.

Poverty is inextricably linked to credibility. The counter-cultural authority of poverty goes hand-in-hand with the counter-cultural authority of the Gospel. This is perhaps one of the chief reasons that the prophetic voice of the Church rings out so clearly from those places where the message of Jesus Christ is experienced as the Good News of freedom for the poor daughters and sons of God.

chastity

If poverty announces freedom from slavery to material things then chastity is good news about the wholesomeness of the human body and the integrity of human relationships. It is also a challenge to remind ourselves of the reality and realism of the Incarnation. Chastity is above all else about right-order in relationships. Like poverty, chastity is counter-cultural. It also issues a challenge to the current discipline of the church from a number of points of view. Does our understanding of sexuality carry the distortions of idolatry and of pre-Christian superstitions and prejudices? Is a Medieval Latin world view responsible for shaping our theory on human sexuality? Is there justification for proposing a universal norm as regards sexual mores? Are practical considerations rather than kingdom values in fact what lie behind the discipline on clerical celibacy that is currently in force? To what extent do we consider medical and scientific progress and technology capable of co-operating with the will of the Creator and to what extent do we see it distorting and disrupting it?

I raise these questions, not with the intention of trying to answer them. (It will be readily acknowledged that each of these issues is an essay – if not a book or a library – in its own right.) Rather, once again, I believe these questions illustrate the climate of tension that surrounds the expectation of virtue surrounding priests in the exercise of their ministry. I still recall the excitement of the debate in the late 1960's and early 1970's when there was much discussion and even anticipation in some quarters, that the normative obligation of celibacy for secular priests was to be discontinued. Although the question was not a pressing one for me personally at that time, (I was still several years away from ordination) I was aware of the discussion leading up to the 1971 announcement that celibacy was to be retained and a sense of disappointment with which it was greeted by many priests. Many of the priests whom I remember waiting for the announcement have since resigned from the ministry and followed other paths. I have often wondered how far their expectation had taken them in a direction that meant that in their own minds they were already living in a Church where the discipline had been changed. To what extent, when the decision was announced did they find it impossible to recover the expectation that they would be celibate for the rest of their lives?

The psychology is complex but, if the analysis is accurate, it perhaps also accounts for what happened in 1968 with the publication of Humanae Vitae. Then too the expectations for change were high and many people had made a life-style commitment which to a large extent was irreversible by the time the document was released. I have no intention of trying to fathom the role of the Holy Spirit. What swayed Pope Paul VI in making the decision he took is not a discussion I wish to pursue here either. However, what strikes me is that public debate in both of these cases surrounding the possibility of change and leading up to an *"authoritative pronouncement"* alters the perception of authority. If there can be two or more sides to an argument then the side upon which the authority comes down will always be open to question by those who feel dissatisfied with the result. Each side inevitably claims that their view is the true one. If only the answer could be found by the employment of Bentham's felicity calculus! But the solution is not to be found by applying in so mathematical a way the methods of empirical science to the arguments put forward. What we are faced with is the problem of reconciling competing theologies in a world of competing cultures.

conflict and good faith

When conflict is rife and tensions grow, Bernard Lonergan's conviction is that the real issue becomes truth.[11] The way we work as human beings is through a process of integrating activities at different levels of awareness to form a dialectic unity in tension.[12] The pastoral presumption when someone approaches the priest to discuss a dilemma in which they find themselves, caused by a conflict between what conclusion the Church understands should be formed from the tension resulting from a dialectic unity and the conclusion others have drawn faced with the same tension, is that the person is in good faith. If theologians and the magisterium have taken time to consider the different sides of an argument then there are considerations that the Church has believed it necessary to take account of before reaching a decision. When the discussion widens beyond the academic-theological traditions that are usually in play in theological and magisterial discussions to take in the wider secular conceptions to which people are generally more exposed, integration is more of a challenge and the tension is usually greater. In fact, sometimes when the underlying philosophies are in conflict the dialectic is incapable of providing even a working resolution to the polarities that are present. Practically speaking this will often mean that people are faced with the choice of accepting one view and discarding the other simply because of the trust they place in the authority at its source.[13]

There is something about the encyclical Humanae Vitae that is significant and telling when we come to consider the issue of authority and governance in the Church. In setting out his understanding of dialogue in Ecclesiam suam, Pope Paul VI created an expectation. The expectation was in line with the renewal being proposed by the Council, with a vision of a Church probing what can be meant by the spirituality of communion and the attendant conversion of institutions and individuals. The way Humanae Vitae was promulgated and received seemed to revert to a prescriptive approach that, all the signs were, was being abandoned. Some of those interviewed in the survey spoke of the prophetic nature of this document. This appears to propose a moral consequentialism that I am sure was not in Paul VI's mind when he wrote the document. I have spent long hours discussing its foundation in reasoned argument. Sometimes it is suggested that its reasons are reasons of faith but this would be to create a dichotomy between faith and reason that I reject. The reception, or rather the widespread rejection of this document, has never really been addressed. It does perhaps teach us an important truth about dialogue – once the expectation that there is going to be dialogue is created there is no going back, for people will expect to be heard and if they believe they are not being listened to they will take their conversation somewhere else.

the trust of the volunteers

I find myself, without having directly addressed any of the questions that I have raised above in relation to the virtue of chastity, at a point where I am convinced that chastity and related questions, whether they be considered as questions of sexuality, gender or abuse, are in a very real way about the trust that *"the volunteers"* are willing to place in those exercising authority and vice-versa. I believe the view expressed by one priest in the survey that *"most people have made up their own minds"* is probably accurate. Many people have taken the conversation somewhere else. If it is the case that most priests find contraception is no longer something most Catholics speak to them about, and I believe this to be so, then it raises questions for me about the trust people have in the priest and in the authoritative teaching of the Church. It is not, it seems to me, a question of understanding but a question of who or what people are willing to trust.

the morale of priests

I wish to consider priestly morale here briefly in the wider context of chastity, not, as some might think because I wish to conclude the discipline of celibacy in itself has a detrimental effect on morale but because the link I have made between chastity and trust is, I believe, a telling one where morale is concerned. The question of the morale of priests is not one that was directly addressed in the NOP survey. However, interpreting some of the responses in the light of my own experience, I consider the morale of priests to be an important issue.

I think this link between chastity and trust is most evident in recent times with regard to the question of sexual abuse. It has meant priests questioning the extent to which they are now trusted by people who at one time would have trusted not only their only lives but also the lives of their children to a priest. It is reassuring to find that many people – indeed probably most of them – still trust the priests they know and who minister to them. Even so, priests themselves, from an institutional point of view know that they have been tarnished by recent disclosures. I feel able to make two observations. Recent experience requires us to look at the whole area of on-going professional formation. Perhaps due to the length of time spent in the formal formational environment of the seminary, many priests seem reluctant to make a commitment to on-going formation. Without the incentive of promotion or salary increases to encourage them, the motivation to make this commitment has to be interior and an integral part of the spirituality of the priest. While the appreciation of what spirituality entails is unclear it is unlikely to provide the necessary motivation. We can find ourselves (and perhaps we already are) in the realms of a vicious circle that means we have no motivation and nothing to motivate us. It maybe that like some alcoholics we will need to hit rock bottom before we come to our senses and start to do something about it.

There is also a desperate need for priests to minister to each other more effectively, with greater trust and openness to provide the support that is needed, especially when we feel under attack, as we sometimes do. More needs to be said and will undoubtedly be said in future about the question of sexual abuse by members of the clergy. However you look at it, it is a cause of great distress for we share in the suffering of the victims and experience the pain of people who are associated with the perpetrators.

The bewilderment and sadness felt by many priests – and I count myself among them – when well regarded and well loved priests suddenly resign from their ministry is also harmful to the morale of those who choose to carry on. The isolation and sense of rejection expressed by some of those who resign is sometimes matched by the feelings of helplessness and loss of those who have known them, worked with them and been their companions. Although it might be argued that it is good for humility, it is hurtful to hear people ask why it's always the good ones who leave. Even without such comments, those who choose to leave have an effect in lowering the morale of those who choose to stay.

The wisdom that comes from our past experience should help us to learn some things for the future. It may be that we priests have never learned to trust each other enough to respond appropriately when difficulties arise. At the same time I am saddened when I think that many of the efforts that are made to create support groups, provide opportunities for ongoing formation and respond to the needs of priests are ignored by those they are intended to support. Although some would say these things should be made *"compulsory"*, the return to compulsion goes against the new climate our vision seeks to establish. Perhaps what we are faced with is a kind of cynicism born of experiences in the past when various initiatives have raised expectations that were dashed. It is much more difficult to motivate and convince disillusioned priests that something can be worthwhile when past expectations have come to nothing. What is offered and the way it is provided, we must surely learn, are important parts of an ongoing dialogue, and essential to the new climate. Methods of adult education have something to teach us in this regard.

support for priests

In one of the other documents that was circulated in preparation for the Cambridge 2000 conference on Authority and Governance in the Catholic Church, *"From Confrontation to Conversation"*, the value of being able to raise and discuss matters of concern in a climate of trust was recognised. The need for trust, for conversation rather than confrontation, is the route we need to take to resolve some of the contentious *"gender issues"*[14] that face both the Church and society at large.

gender issues

Recently (1999) the Catholic bishops of Scotland undertook a survey of parishes to discover the extent of lay participation. One of the facts to emerge was that it is women who are playing the

173

greatest part in the various areas of the lay apostolate, in supporting the mission of the Church in the parishes. Happily, the survey also showed that the vast majority of priests make no distinction in encouraging lay men and lay women to be involved. That fact that women seem more willing to become involved does, however, mean that the gender issues facing both the Church and society at large are very much *"live"* issues for priests. Alleged attempts to restrict, if not exclude altogether, women's involvement in seminary formation as well as being ill-advised would seem to be becoming increasingly impossible. There is still much room for improvement but there has also been much progress.

relationships and authority

Chastity, understood as a sign of the Kingdom, given by the whole community of faith, would be a witness to trust and shared responsibility in a suspicious world. If trust and responsibility are involved, it goes without saying that this has implications for how we perceive the exercise of authority. It is about relationships between laity, religious and clergy, about how men and women in the Church regard each other. Whether in terms of this particular rhetoric or in terms of the issues it points to is immaterial; how we understand and experience chastity, it seems to me is something we have to face up to if the ministry of the Church of the future is to be truly collaborative. A broader historical and cultural perspective is important for a dialogue that is long overdue concerning human sexuality – one that is not driven by an obsession with the physical as many of the current contributions seem to be, but one that appreciates better what being sexual persons means for the work of spreading the Gospel.

obedience

I have already indicated above that obedience first and foremost means listening to God. In a classical appreciation of the three virtues, obedience is the one that would most readily be associated with the exercise of authority and governance. I have heard more than one experienced priest say that as ordination approached his main concern was with the promise of celibacy. However, after several years the most difficult commitment to live out is obedience. The promise of obedience made by the priest to the bishop is a moment of intimacy during the ceremony of ordination. Kneeling before the bishop the priest places his hands in the hands of the bishop and in response to the question *"Do you promise respect and obedience to me and my successors?"* he replies *"I do"*.

Applied in a restrictive, authoritarian way, obedience takes freedom away. Yet a tradition that reaches back to Christ, and even further to Abraham, has repeatedly presented the obedience of faith as the greatest expression of freedom possible. The exercise of authority over someone who has given a promise of obedience places enormous, godlike demands on the authority figure. In actual fact, the responsibility lies far less with the one under obedience than with the one under authority.

Curiously, whenever the discussion about an appointments board comes up among most of the priests I speak to, they are unconvinced about the value of a number of others assisting the bishop in this aspect of his ministry. One of the bishops in the survey says he finds the appointment of priests the most difficult part of his ministry. At the same time other bishops, I know, find the discussions they have with priests at this time in the vast majority of cases confirm the great generosity of the priests, as well as their obedience, in their readiness to undertake great upheaval, in every sense, in keeping with the will of the bishop for the good of the diocese.

As far as the suggestion that lay people could have a greater say in the appointment of priests is concerned, I believe many of the points raised in the survey accurately reflect the current attitude of priests. There is at least anecdotal evidence to suggest that in the Church of Scotland successive ministers sometimes swing from one attitude to the other and that the Kirk Session is often seen as being responsible for this. So, for example, if the out-going minister has a great interest in social justice and community issues an effort will be made to ensure that his successor is more interested in caring for the fabric of the church's property. As with all anecdotes there may be a tendency to caricature in this, but it would nevertheless be true to say that the continuity and respect for the needs of the parish that lay involvement in appointments might be hoped to secure would not always necessarily result.

One of the bishops interviewed raises the issue of the extent to which lay involvement in appointment of priests is a challenge to

clergy appointments

accountability

the role of the hierarchy as set out by Christ. Many of the other issues discussed surrounding this question of appointments seemed to me to be about practical matters. This comment does seem to raise a question that relates to the experience of competing theologies that I have already spoken about. It again points to the tension that priests are living with. To whom (under Christ) is the priest ultimately accountable? The priest today can find that both the bishop and the people have expectations that are sometimes in conflict. The priest, for example, can find he is given an appointment to a parish where the perception from the point of view of the bishop and his advisors is that the parish should be prepared for closure, whereas the people see the new priest as one who is coming to champion their cause of saving the parish. It does not take a great deal of imagination (or depth of knowledge) to recognise many other situations where the priest will find himself caught in the middle.

Although there is evidence to suggest that the Bishop and the diocesan authorities are often felt to be distant from the parish, they can play a significant part in the life of the parish, especially, as has been noted, at the time of the appointment of priests.[15] There can also be upheaval when the bishop is changed. When the diocese has been led in one direction for several years and then a new man comes along and changes everything with no consultation the anger and resentment is understandable and justified.

a hierarchical or a communitarian approach

These, however, are only symptoms of what I would regard as a much deeper ecclesiological issue in which the tension is evident. The governance of the Roman Catholic Church has always been considered to be hierarchical. A preference for what might be termed a more *"communitarian"* model has emerged in some places in recent years. Even where this latter model is in evidence priests still find they are in effect working both models at the same time. It is not easy to imagine what needs to be done to address this situation both in terms of its effect on the morale of priests and in trying to see if a theologically adequate synthesis of the two models might be possible and of benefit for the future governance of the Church.

I am not sure how this synthesis might be arrived at or what it might be, or indeed whether such a synthesis might be the way forward for the Church. In faithfulness to the general thrust of this paper, however, it would seem that dialogue has something to offer. I have drawn attention to the fact that priests are ministering in the midst of a tension caused by competing ecclesiologies. If, as I suggested already, those to whom obedience is owed have a greater responsibility than the one who submits in obedience, then whether the one in authority is the bishop or the community, they have a great deal of responsibility towards the priest – a responsibility to understand what he faces because of their expectations and a responsibility to keep the demands they make under constant review to ensure they are reasonable.

having reasonable expectations

The only way of respecting all the people who are living in the midst of this tension, people, bishops and priests, would seem to be the way of dialogue. In the short and medium term dialogue is incredibly unproductive as far as the task to be performed is concerned. It calls for meetings to take place, for diaries to be compared, for decisions to be reached over a much longer period of time. It can be frightening, for when we sit down to dialogue the world can seem to be running away from us. Taking the long term view puts a different complexion on things. There is great truth in the popular saying *"act in haste, repent at leisure"*, for it is not unknown for those who feel their concerns, values or opinions have been ignored to sabotage the decision from which they have been excluded. Even when sabotage does not take place, those who feel excluded will sometimes simply walk away. We owe it to the future to make dialogue part of the culture of the present for the sake of the future, for the obedience of volunteers will only be at best half-hearted if their love for what they committed themselves to is not honoured and given due consideration.

dialogue and the long term view

In seeking to draw closer to the truth and to enjoy the freedom this gives, priests themselves also have a responsibility to allow themselves to be ministered to by people, the bishops and their fellow priests. In many cases we have to learn to do this from the start, for in some respects the image of the priest according to which formation has taken place is of the one who is invulnerable, who needs nothing from anyone and has everything to give. This image owes more to the gods of Mount Olympus or the Nietzschean *"superman"* than the Good Shepherd. An appreciation of what poverty, chastity and obedience entail in a Church of communion is likely to project the

ministering to the minister

openness, the humility, the willingness to be corrected and the trust in the goodness of others that the Gospel expects of true disciples. This, after all, was one of the great lessons St. Peter had to learn before Christ entrusted him with the responsibilities of leadership. Peter's reluctance to allow the Master to wash his feet was almost his undoing.[16] Unless priests learn that they too must allow those to whom they owe obedience to be Christ for them there will be no hope of resolving the tensions or even of living with them. Peter who is sometimes portrayed as impulsive and stubborn learned the lesson, as we are reminded in Paul's letter to the Galatians. He was challenged by Paul at Antioch and revised his position accordingly.[17]

the seminary

The willingness to be ministered to in a context of dialogue is essential if formation programmes are to be effective. Until fairly recently I was a staff member for many years in the seminary and was often aware that an appreciation of the seminary as a place where the seminarian was being ministered to was sadly lacking. This may have had much to do with the system, as has been suggested in the survey. The attitude to assessment meant that for a number of students dialogue was out of the question. Staff members were regarded by some with suspicion, more as assessors than fellow pilgrims, as teachers rather than disciples. While I recall with a great deal of fondness my own time as a seminarian, when I was certainly ministered to by my fellow seminarians and by priests and others who were in positions of responsibility, I do not remember dialogue being part of our vocabulary. At the same time there were some experiences of group decision-making and taking but also an understanding that those in authority knew best what was good for us. I would also maintain that the vast majority of the colleagues who worked alongside me during the time I was a staff member – whether they were lay, religious or priests – were convinced that what they were offering the seminarians was ministry and they did so with great conviction, expertise and generosity. Yet, it would only be honest to admit that to a large extent the model of authority and governance we fell into took a paternalistic approach that was prepared to hear what students thought but was generally convinced that we knew best.

In acknowledging the responsibility of seminary staffs for failing to promote a climate of dialogue as effectively as might have been done, there is a more general cultural phenomenon that militates against trustful conversation. The great philosophical axiom, *"quidiquid recipitur per modum recipientis recipitur"* (whatever is received is received according to the receivers way of receiving) is perhaps apposite here. If there is suspicion and resistance to accepting the ministry that is offered, even though it may be inadequate, it is difficult to make progress in the direction of dialogue. The great sadness about this is that those who develop a habit of resisting in seminary are also unlikely to perceive the importance of formation that continues after ordination. The attitude of the *"stand-off"* all too easily persists.

The model of obedience that is in play here is significant for in seminaries too the competing theologies are operative. Obedience understood as conforming to a code of behaviour that is characterised by a *"jumping-through-hoops"* mentality often operates side by side with an approach that seeks to promote a more interior understanding of obedience as a listening to God, to oneself, to one's peers and to those in authority. It often happens that when someone is considered to be failing to embrace obedience in this latter sense the seminary authorities are asked to base a final assessment on whether or not the seminarian is capable of jumping through a number of well defined hoops. The tension that comes from trying to operate these competing models together leaves the seminary in the same situation as the rest of the Church. Dialogue, while not always capable of achieving the often desired measurable results is nevertheless the only obvious path leading to something better.

competing theologies

As far as continuing formation is concerned there are certainly some priests who are convinced of its importance and go out of their way to make use of the opportunities provided. Others, however, are either living proof of the proverb that you can take the horse to water but you can't force it to drink or frightening examples of how the individualism of the age has also infected many priests. I have already stated my view that compulsion is not the answer.

continuing formation

What one recently ordained priest said about appraisal is probably what some would also say about continuing formation in general.

"Perhaps appraisal, but I'm so fed up after being in the seminary all that time, you just want to be left to be yourself..... Personal lives should remain personal unless personal lives become a problem. They then become accountable. Accountability should only be in relation to your doing priestly things." I am drawn to the image of an exasperated Jesus as he is portrayed in the Gospel of Matthew, where his efforts to convince the Scribes and Pharisees in particular of the importance of his message are constantly meeting stony opposition: *"We played the pipes for you, and you wouldn't dance; we sang dirges, and you wouldn't be mourners."*[18] He knew the tension too. It is not a new phenomenon but has to be addressed anew, with imagination and creativity in every generation, for it takes different forms.

a commitment to dialogue

If, as I have suggested here, there are new ways of facing tensions if we understand and live out poverty, chastity and obedience as expressions of a spirituality of communion, the paralysis of having to take account of too many questions can be overcome. These counsels, as the marks of virtue, need not be seen as the straitjacket of uniformity. The variety of gifts and the range of responsibilities present in the Church mean that what the Gospel counsels in terms of poverty, chastity and obedience, is different for different people but part of the one richness. The tensions should make us uncomfortable and dissatisfied with the present and strain forward to the future. The conversations we enter into because of our commitment to dialogue are part of the strain. The energy that was spent on the asceticism of the past needs to be devoted to what is needed for today. Pope Paul VI spoke of going in new ways almost 40 years ago when he took office during the Council: *"In the dialogue one discovers how different are the ways which lead to the light of faith, and how it is possible to make them converge on the same goal. Even if these ways are divergent, they can become complementary by forcing our reasoning process out of the worn paths and by obliging it to deepen its research, to find fresh expressions."*[19]

It is sometimes frightening to discover there are so many expectations, so many questions and so many roads along which the answers seem to lie. Hope for many of us, I think, comes at times not from our ability to find the answers or even from a conviction that the answers will be found, but from hoping against hope, and by our willingness to be here to hope against hope, by touching the lives, the sometimes hopeless lives of others in unforgettable ways and by allowing them to come close enough to touch us in ways that we also will never forget. This describes a dialogue founded on love and the belief that where there is love there is always hope. Allowing those we are learning to love to draw close, albeit often reluctantly, through dialogue, it is possible, with the help of God, to incarnate together a community of virtue that disarms suspicion and opens the door to trust.

[1] Shakespeare, Measure for Measure, II, ii
[2] I use the word in the same sense as Timms – not to mean *"verbal fireworks but the significant words in public argument used to state a position and convince an audience"*, as pointed out in his reference to Billig, 1987.
[3] Ecclesiam suam, on the church in our day, 6 August, 1964
[4] Decree on the Ministry and Life of Priests, Presbyterorum Ordinis, 7 December 1965.
[5] Dogmatic Constitution of the Church, Vatican II, 21 November, 1964
[6] Pastoral Constitution on the Church in the Modern World, Vatican II, 7 December 1965.
[7] Insight, p. 639, DLT, 1983
[8] Matthew 23:4
[9] This may seem a rather naïve view, especially if the observations of Fr. Donald Cozzens in his book The Changing Face of the Priesthood, (Collegeville, 2000) are accurate. However, even what he has to say can only be appreciated if it is understood against a background of expectation and commitment to a virtuous way of life that are part of a patrimony built up by generations of priests who have proclaimed the Gospel of Jesus Christ not only in what they say but by the way they have lived.
[10] Decree on the Ministry and Life of Priests, 17
[11] Insight, p.549
[12] Lonergan holds this to be the case and goes on to say "it follows: 1) that the intellectual activities are either the proper unfolding of the detached and disinterested desire to know or else a distorted unfolding due to the interference of other desire, and 2) that the sensitive activities, from which intellectual contents emerge and in which they are represented, expressed, and applied, either are involved in the mysteries of the proper unfolding or distort these mysteries into myths. Insight, p.548.
[13] Lonergan, in his analysis of belief (Insight pp.707 ff.), points out that our acceptance of truth can be based on belief that is more an act of the will than an act of intellect. It is important to recognise that claiming to know something to be true is quite different from claiming to believe it is true. (p. 718)
[14] At the Cambridge 2000 conference, Professor Mary Grey and Professor Joe Selling gave a presentation during which they made a case for speaking not

so much about sexuality but rather about gender. In this way, they suggested, our perspective would be a much wider one and could help us to resolve questions that presently seem to be insoluble.

[15] This emerged quite clearly from parish and diocesan surveys and interviews carried out in preparation for the Cambridge 2000 Conference on Authority and Governance in the Roman Catholic Church.

[16] John 13:6-8

[17] Galatians 2:11 ff

[18] Matthew 11:17

[19] Ecclesiam suam, 83

Appendix One

RESEARCH TOPIC GUIDE

A INTRODUCTION

1 Introduce NOP Business
   MRS Code of Conduct: confidentiality and anonymity
   Explain use of tape recorder

2 Background to the research: to explore views of authority and governance in the Roman Catholic Church.

3 Respondent profile:
   - name
   - brief background and current position
   - year of ordination (as appropriate)
   - year of resignation of active ministry (as appropriate)

B PRIESTHOOD

1 I would like to ask you first about your understanding of priesthood.
   What does priesthood mean to you?

2 What led/leads you to seek holy orders?

3 What were your expectations at that time?

4 *(All except seminarians)* To what extent have those expectations been met?

5 To what extent do you see your ministry as functional (for example, **parish maintenance**)?

6 And to what extent do you see your ministry as having a deeper significance within the Christian community?

7 Do you believe that holy orders changes you in some way, or not?

8 *(If yes)* In what way does holy orders change you?

9 Do you believe that holy orders distinguishes an individual from the common priesthood of all the baptised, or not? In what way?

10 *(Ask if yes or no to Q.9)* What are the consequences of this belief for you and the nature of your ministry?

11 How would you describe your model of the church? *(If necessary, give examples of servant, pilgrim)*

12 How do you endeavour to put this model into practice?

13 To what extent do you see yourself as the manager of a parish?

14 Do/did you feel that the Seminary provides you with the skills necessary to manager a parish, or not?

15 How do you feel you are/were viewed by your parishioners? Is this important to you, or not?

16 What kind of future are you trying to bring about?

17 Are you optimistic, or pessimistic, about the future? Why is this?

18 What do you see as the main problems facing the church as this time?

19 And what would you say are the main opportunities for the church at this time?

C GOVERNANCE

1 Do you believe that only priests have competence to govern in the church, or is this something that lay people could also do? Why do you say this?

2 Is it appropriate in your view that only priests should govern?

3 Is it just that only priests should govern?

4 How satisfied are you with the quality of government in the contemporary church? At different levels?

5 Do you have any concerns about government in the church, or not? *(If yes)* What are your major concerns?

6 What changes, if any, would you like to see in government in the church?

7 What part should lay people play in the government of the church? At parish level? At Vatican level?

8   In cases where a lay person is more professionally qualified – and professional judgement is required – should the lay person be able to overrule the parish priest? Why do you say this?

9   The Churches in the British Isles has recently been scandalised by cases of child abuse. Are you satisfied with the way the church has dealt with them, or not? Why do you say this?

10 Why do you think such cases happen? In your view, what are the causes?

11 What remedies would you propose?

D   AUTHORITY

1   *(Show Card 1)* I would now like you to indicate whether you believe each individual/organisation on this list exercises too much or too little authority.

2   What would you say distinguishes your authority as an ordained minister from the authority of a lay Christian?

3   What authority would you claim, that you believe could not, or should not, be claimed by a lay person?

4   What roles would you say are appropriate to lay people in the church?

5   *(Show Card 2)* On this card are several statements about the role of lay people in the church. I would like you to read through all of them, and then tell me to what extent you agree or disagree with them, using a scale of 1 to 10, where 1 = completely disagree, and 10 = fully agree.

6   Which of these is closest to your own views? Why is this?

7   And which of these is furthest from your own views? Why is this?

8   Should priests and bishops be accountable?

9   If yes, to whom? If no, why not?

10 Do you believe you have adequate influence over the appointment of your bishop?

11 What influence do you, in fact, have?

12 Should lay people participate more fully in:
- the selection of candidates for the priesthood
- the appointment of priests
- the appointment of bishops?

13 Are you in favour of women in key decision making position in the church: For example:
- nuns or lay women as Heads of Vatican Congregations?
- women a judges in marriage tribunals
- women involved in the appointment of priests or bishops?

E   FORMATION

1 *(Ask all except seminarians)* Looking back now, how relevant would you say the formation you received was?

(Ask seminarians) How appropriate do you think your formation is as preparation for your future responsibilities in the church?

2 If you were responsible for formation, what changes, if any, would you introduce?

3 Is sufficient attention given to **human** (rather than priestly) formation? What do you think of providing formation in the following areas *(show Card 3)*:
- relationships
- child protection
- communication skills
- groupwork/teamwork skills
- working collaboratively
- chaplaincy training
- finance
- administration

4 In your view, are areas like these currently a fashionable obsession, or crucial for the church of the future?

5 What about continuing formation? How satisfactory is it, at present?

6 What do you see as the most urgent priorities?

7 Should lay people participate in the continuing formation of

priests? In what ways?

8 How do you feel about the idea of priests and lay people attending courses together, for example at seminaries, or in the diocese?

9 Do you feel that you have adequate influence over your own "career" in the church?

10 How do you feel about a *"professional"* model being applied to your role as a priest? Is it an appropriate model, or not?

11 Should a priest be concerned with issues like:
   - assessment/appraisal
   - career development
   - accountability

12 Why do you say this?

F ISSUES FACING THE CHURCH

1 I would not like to ask for your views about some of the more controversial issues facing the church today. Please tell me your personal attitude towards current teaching **on any of these you are willing to discuss.** *(Show Card 4)*

2 Is it your view that the boundaries of orthodoxy are being drawn more tightly, or not?

3 Rome has suggested that some of these issues are closed for discussion. What would be your response if approached by lay people or colleagues for advice and help on these matters?

4 What place has *"loyal dissent"* in the church?

5 Are you satisfied that those who question church teaching are given a fair hearing, or not? Why do you say this?

6 What action, if any, is necessary in this area?

7 How would you respond if the instruction you received from your Bishop contradicted what the Pope was teaching?

G CONCLUSION

1 Is there anything else you would like to add on the subject of authority and governance in the Roman Catholic Church?

2   Thank you very much for your participation. May I re-emphasise that all your responses will be treated in confidence, and you will not be identified in the research report, or in the book it is hoped will be published as part of this research.

3   Finally, would you have any objection to our sharing the tape recording of this interview with others from Queen's College, Birmingham who are involved in this research?

Thank you again for your participation in this research

CARD 1

Do the following exercise too little, the right amount, or too much authority?
(Please tick one box for each)

	Too little	Right amount	Too much
• The College of Bishops			
• Heads of diocesan departments (e.g. Diocesan Financial Secretary)			
• Curial officials			
• Cardinal Hume (in Scotland: Cardinal Winning)			
• Lay people			
• Heads of the Curial Congregations			
• You as a priest			
• The Pope			
• The College of Cardinals			
• Your diocesan Bishop			

CARD 2

Please indicate to what extent you agree or disagree with the following statements, using a scale of 1 to 10, where:

1 = completely disagree
10 = fully agree

                                                                            Rating

- Jesus entrusted the mission of the church to bishops and priests. The laity's role is to support and **assist** them.

- The role of lay Christians is to act as a bridge between Christ's Church and the world, to be **sign** of God's love in the world.

- Lay people are called to **transform the world**, make it good: to heal it of sin, develop it and prepare it for Christ's second coming.

- Lay people are partners with the hierarchy in the mission of the church and should participate with them in teaching, ministry and church administration.

- Lay people do not have a role in the church. They are the church! The question is, rather, what is the special role of the ordained minister.

CARD 3

SHOULD FORMATION INCLUDE ...

- relationships

- child protection

- communication skills

- groupwork/teamwork skills

- working collaboratively

- chaplaincy training

- finance

- administration

CARD 4

ISSUES FACING THE CHURCH

– Celibacy

– Offering communion to Christians of other denominations

– Women priests

– Contraception

– The validity of Anglican orders

– Married priests

– Sacramental participation of the divorced

Appendix Two

SELECTED FINDINGS FROM AN AMERICAN SURVEY

The report of the 1993 Survey of Catholic Priests in America (Hoge, Shields and Griffin) was based on the results of returns of 1,186 postal questionnaires (a response rate of almost 70%). After a two fold weighting the researchers claim that *"our data comes as close as possible to representing all American priests"* (p.3). The purposes of the survey – partly concerned with replication of earlier studies, partly interested in presbyterical councils – and its methods were clearly different from the present study. However, some of the questions posed do at least touch on those raised in the study of authority and governance. These are presented below, so that the range of opinion can be illustrated. Most of the questions are relevant to chapter one. In the summary responses quoted agree strongly and agree somewhat have been amalgamated as have disagree strongly and disagree somewhat. Similarly with 'problem' and 'no problem'.

Ecclesiological and Theological Issues

	% Agree	% Disagree	% Uncertain
There is no ontological difference between the priest and the laity, since all share in the common priesthood of Christ given at baptism; the difference is mainly one of assigned duties	26	67	7
The idea that the priest is 'a man set apart' is a barrier to the full realisation of true Christian community	28	63	9
I feel I am most a priest when I am 'saying' mass and hearing confessions	70	26	4
Priests today need to be more involved with broad social and moral issues beyond the parish level	72	11	17

Problems Facing Priests

	% Problem	% No Problem
The way authority is exercised in the Church	67	33
Unrealistic demands and expectations of lay people	57	43
Being expected to represent Church teachings I have difficulty with	46	55
Celibacy	43	57
Theological change in the concept of priesthood	36	64
Uncertainty about the future of the Church	39	61

Appendix 3

THE AUTHORITY AND GOVERNANCE PROJECT

Established in 1996 at the Queen's Ecumenical Foundation for Theological Education, Birmingham, this initiative is concerned with the nature, exercise and experience of authority and the practise of government in the Roman Catholic Church. The backround to the project is set out in *From Confrontation to Conversation*, a brief consultation document available from the Foundation. The aims are to assist the Church address the complex problems of authority, governance, relationships and participation in contemporary Britain and, where appropriate, adapt pastoral policy and practice. These include a desire to distinguish the authority that is a baptismal right and responsibility from that which follows from orders and office in the Church. Implications for the lay baptismal vocation are a particular concern.

A conversational methodology has been adopted – open, generous and respectful – drawing upon the views and experience of bishops, priests, theologians and ordinary lay Catholics. About 1000 people have been consulted. Special attention has been given to those groups whose circumstances lead them to experience the authority of the Church more acutely than others e.g. the divorced, those married to Christians of other denominations, ethnic minorities, priests and religious no longer active in ministry and women. The project involves empirical enquiry, theological reflection, publication and dissemination at local level within the Church.

The research has been directed by a specialist working party. The members are able to offer expertise in theology, philosophy, social science, church and business administration.

In addition to the bishops, priests and seminarians who participated in the NOP survey upon which this book is based, the Queen's Foundation has enjoyed the generous co-operation of a number of dioceses, educational institutions and membership organisations within the Church. Six dioceses collaborated in preparing a series of diocesan and parish case studies. These examine how bishops, with their advisors and key personnel, endeavour to make the best use of the scarce human and financial resources available to them in addressing issues of pastoral strategy, organisation and communication. They also explore the reality at parish level. Edited by Professor Noel Timms, with commentaries from two theologians, a sociologist an accountant and an organisation specialist, the results have been published by Matthew James under the title *Diocesan Dispositions and Parish Voices*.

Sarum College, Salisbury, in association with the Queen's Foundation, held two residential seminars for theologians and social scientists to discuss the delicate issues of authority, sexuality and relationships in the Catholic tradition. The experience and understanding of sexuality have changed markedly in recent decades and the ethical concerns to which these changes give rise touch the lives of all, both within and outside the Church. The Sarum seminars examined the conceptions of sexuality and relationship which inform Church teaching and the extent to which teaching might take account of change whilst remaining faithful to Christian tradition. *Embracing Sexuality: The Church's Teaching and the Experience of her People*, based upon papers presented at the seminars and edited by Professor Joseph Selling, will be published by Ashgate in spring 2001.

ADVENT, the support group for priests and religious (both male and female) who are no longer in active ministry, the Association of Divorced and Separated Catholics, the Association of Interchurch Families, the Catholic Association for Racial Justice and the Margaret Beaufort Institute, Cambridge, all contributed to the Authority and Governance Project, drawing upon the experience of their members and contacts. The results of two studies have been published; others will follow.

A Painful Process, by Andrew Bebb and Anna Roper, is published by Matthew James with a commentary by Professor James O'Connell. It summarises the outcome of an investigation into the experience and aspirations of a sample of ADVENT members subsequent to their resignation from active ministry.

Outcaste To Authority is published by the Catholic Association for Racial Justice. Based upon extensive consultation it addresses questions of authority, governance and participation in the Church from the point of view of ethnic minorities.

The Association of Interchurch Families has completed a study of authority and eucharistic sharing in interchurch families. The Margaret Beaufort Institute has examined employment structures and the experiences of lay women engaged in ministerial roles in the Church.

In addition to empirical enquiries, the Queen's Foundation has also commissioned three collections of papers.

Governance and Authority In The Roman Catholic Church: Beginning a Conversation, is edited by Professor Noel Timms and Dr. Kenneth Wilson and published by SPCK. The book explores specific problems facing the Roman Catholic Church in the twentieth century from the points of view of theology and social science.

Authority in the Roman Catholic Church: Theory and Practice, edited by Dr. Bernard Hoose continues the work begun in the previous volume with an emphasis on historical and theological reflection. It raises such questions as "What form of authority should exist in the Church of Christ, where is it to be found and how should it be exercised?" The book will be published by Ashgate in the autumn of 2001.

A Thematic Reader on Authority and Governance in the Roman Catholic Church, is edited by Dr. Gerard Mannion, Professor Richard Gaillardetz, Professor Jan Kerkhofs and Dr. Kenneth Wilson. As the title suggests, the reader is a collection of seminal writing essential to an informed understanding of authority and governance in the Church. It includes extracts from key church documents and papal pronouncements. The reader will be published by Ashgate in the autumn of 2001.

To promote informed discussion of the issues, the Queen's Foundation will establish a dedicated web-site and will work with Matthew James Publishing to develop appropriate resource materials for schools and parishes.

Bibliography

Ashford, S. and Timms, N. *What Europe Thinks*
    Dartmouth, Aldershot

Beiner, R. (1983) *Political Judgment*
    Methuen, London

Billig, M. (1987) *Arguing and Thinking*
    Cambridge University Press, Cambridge

Butler, C. (1999) ed. *Faith, Hope and Chastity*
    Harper Collins Religious, London

Cornwell, J. (1999) *Hitler's Pope*
    Viking, Harmondsworth

Doohan, L. (1984) *The Lay Centred Church, Theology and Spirituality*
    Winston Press Minneapolis

Duffy, E. (1966) *'Priests for Ever'*
    Priests and People, June 1996, pp. 217 – 221

Emmet, D. (1972) *Function, Purpose and Power*
    Macmillan, London

George, F. (1999) *'Episcopal Conferences: Theological Bases'*
    Communio 26, pp. 393-409

Hemrick, E. and Hoge, D. (1991) *A Survey of Priests Ordained Five to Nine Years*
    Seminary Dept. of the National Catholic Educational Association

Hoge, D., Shields, J., and Griffin, D. (1993) *Survey of Catholic Priests on Leadership and Priestly Life*
    National Federation of Priests' Councils, Washington

Hoose, B. ed (forthcoming) *Authority in the Roman Catholic Church: Theory and Practice*
Ashgate, London

Hornsby-Smith, M. (1989) *The Changing Parish*
Routledge, London

Lonergan, B., S.J. (1972) *Method in Theology*
Darton, Longman and Todd, London

Machiavelli, N. (1988) *The Prince*
Bell, London. Bohn's Standard Library

Mason, K. (1992) *Priesthood and Society*
Canterbury Press, Norwich

Oakeshott, M. (1962) *Rationalism in Politics*
Methuen, London
(1989) *The Voice of Liberal Learning*
ed. T. Fuller, Yale University
(1993) *Religion, Politics and the Moral Life*
ed. T. Fuller, Yale University Press, New Haven and London

Plant, R. (1974) *Community and Ideology*
Routledge and Kegan Paul, London

Polanyi, M. (1958) *Personal Knowledge: towards a post-critical philosophy*
Routledge and Kegan Paul, London

Timms, N. (1992) *Family and Citizenship*
Dartmouth, Aldershot
(2001) *Diocesan Dispositions and Parish Voices*
Matthew James, Chelmsford